Ghost House Books

First printed in 2002 10 9 8 7 6 5 4 3 2 1
Printed in Canada

The Publisher: Ghost House Books
Distributed by Lone Pine Publishing
10145 – 81 Avenue
Edmonton, AB T6E 1W9
Canada

Website: http://www.ghostbooks.net

National Library of Canada Cataloguing in Publication Data
Christensen, Jo-Anne.
Haunted hotels

ISBN 1-894877-03-9

1. Haunted hotels. 2. Ghosts. I. Title.
BF1474.5.C47 2002 133.1'22 C2002-910514-5

Editorial Director: Nancy Foulds
Project Editor: Shelagh Kubish
Editorial: Shelagh Kubish, Chris Wangler
Illustrations Coordinator: Carol Woo
Production Coordinator: Jennifer Fafard
Book Design: Jeff Fedorkiw
Cover Design: Rod Michalchuk, Elliot Engley
Layout & Production: Jeff Fedorkiw
Photo Credits: Every effort has been made to accurately credit photographers. Any errors or omissions should be directed to the publisher for changes in future editions. The photographs in the book are reproduced with the generous permission of their owners: Austin History Center, Austin Public Library PICA 05020 (p. 171); Biltmore Hotel (p. 166, p. 168); Bullock Hotel (p. 90); Centennial Archives, Deadwood Public Library (p. 86); Dalhousie Castle (p. 194); Dryburgh Abbey Hotel (p. 203); Echo Valley Conference Center (p. 104, p. 105); Hotel del Coronado (p. 12, p. 14); Hotel Queen Mary (p. 23); Manresa Castle (p. 76); Museum of New Mexico, negative #11040 (p. 133); negative #10464 (p. 134); Oregon Historical Society, #OrHi 39576 (p. 63); Rama Patel (p. 150); Pfister Hotel (p. 115, p. 116); Moira Pitt (p. 212); La Posada de Santa Fe (p. 132); Provincial Archives of Manitoba, negative #W9341 (p. 127); Barbara Smith (p. 39, p. 43); Yukon Archives. H.C. Barley Collection, #5039 (p. 57).

We acknowledge the financial support of the Government of Canada through the Book Publishing Industry Development Program (BPIDP) for our publishing activities.

PC: P6

DEDICATION

For Evelyn Vivian Arnold,
the newest guest to check into this big hotel

Chapter IV—Spirits of the South

Chapter V—Britain's Ghostly Guests

Acknowledgments

This book involved an extensive amount of research, which took place over a period of several years. In the end, the material I collected came from, literally, hundreds of different sources. I therefore owe hundreds of thank yous—which I will now present in a manageable and abbreviated form.

To everyone whose name is mentioned within the body of the text—if I have quoted you from an interview or from a written work—please accept my thanks for your contribution to this project. Other "behind-the-scenes" people deserve special mention here. They include Lori Herndier, Echo Valley Conference Centre; Mercy Hague and Troy Love, Bullock Hotel; Lauren Ash Donoho, Hotel del Coronado; Robin Wachner, Hotel *Queen Mary;* Royal Alcott and Jack Moyer, the Crescent Hotel; Anne Bingham, La Posada de Santa Fe; Jennifer Clearwater, Ellingsen and Brady Advertising and Public Relations; G.W. Earle, Earle Hotels; the Ptolemy family, Comlongon Castle; Neville Petts, Dalhousie Castle; Cathy Griffon, the Talbot; Jeanette Lundquist, Deadwood Public Library; and Moira Pitt of British Columbia.

Other unsung heroes who deserve thanks are the many kind and helpful people with whom I dealt at countless museums, libraries and historical societies throughout North America and Great Britain. Here, closer to home, two people who were of invaluable assistance were my dear friend and fellow author, Barbara Smith, and the talented writer, researcher and lecturer, W. Ritchie Benedict.

For their talents, enthusiasm and professionalism, I also thank the management and staff of Ghost House

Books. It is a true pleasure to work with all of you—I could not imagine a more perfect relationship.

Finally, as always, I am grateful to and for my family—my husband, Dennis, and my children, Steven, Grace, William and Natalie. Without your support, none of this would be possible. You are all my lucky stars and I love you.

Introduction

I love staying in hotels.

And I *love* a good ghost story.

You can imagine my delight when one evening in 1995 I saw a television program about a beautiful spirit who was known to be haunting a luxurious Santa Fe hotel (La Posada de Santa Fe, page 131). When the show ended, I was left wondering whether there might be more haunted hotels out there. Today, I honestly wonder whether there are any hotels that are not home to a specter or two.

In *The Shining*, a novel set in an eerily vacant resort hotel, Stephen King wrote, "...every big hotel has got a ghost. Why? Hell, people come and go. Sometimes one of 'em will pop off in his room, heart attack or stroke or something like that. Hotels are superstitious places..."

They're often historical places too, and ghost stories have a way of complementing and enhancing history. Of course, not every hotel manager views the spirits in such a positive light. Many still fear that talk of a ghost will drive away business (quite the opposite appears to be true), and they refuse to publicly admit to a haunting. Sometimes, the "official word" on a ghost story will change along with a change of ownership or management. Three hotels that had been enthusiastically involved with this project at the beginning requested in recent months that their stories be withdrawn. In each case, I can guarantee you that the ghosts didn't leave—but the original management did.

Most hoteliers, however, recognize that a ghost is a valuable link to the history of their establishment. People are fascinated by and drawn to haunted hotels, and, statistically, very few are ever frightened away.

I do have three notes that are worthy of mention:

One—this is not a travel guide. I accept no responsibility for your disappointment should you try to check into the Kootenay Hotel, which burned down in 1969, or the Goldfield, which hasn't registered a paying guest since the last world war.

Two—this is not a comprehensive collection. It is a collection of my favorite stories. There are so many haunted hotels out there, it would be impossible to document them all in one volume—or, for that matter, in ten.

And, three—if you notice a variation in storytelling style between North America and Great Britain, understand that it reflects a variation in history, culture and attitude. In Britain, the buildings and the ghost stories both tend to be ancient and it follows that the story details are sketchier; they tell more like legends. They are every bit as intriguing, however, and just plain off the scale in terms of atmosphere.

Now, the moment has come to sign the guest register and check into a time when hotels were grand enough to be considered vacation destinations in themselves. It's a journey made possible by a few ghostly guides...Don't mind the bellman; he tends to vanish the moment you turn your back...

Welcome to these Haunted Hotels—I do hope you enjoy your stay.

CHAPTER 1
Golden State Ghosts

Hotel Del Coronado

It had long been rumored that the magnificent Hotel del Coronado was haunted. In the early 1990s, the hosts of a morning show on a local radio station heard some of those whispered stories and realized that they had the makings of a unique Halloween special. They arranged to broadcast their program live from the reputedly haunted room on the morning of October 31.

Not that they really believed in the ghost. They just thought that it might be entertaining.

A docent at the hotel named Barbara Perkins filled them in on the legend and arranged for the announcers and their engineer to have the room on the night before the broadcast. It was agreed that Perkins would join them for an interview during the following morning's show.

The special Halloween broadcast had been heavily promoted for a week. But when Perkins arrived at the room prior to 6 AM, as requested, she found that the announcers had abandoned the idea and gone back to the radio station. The only person remaining was the sound engineer, who had been left behind to pack up the equipment. When Perkins walked in the room, he looked up at her with darkly circled eyes that clearly had not closed all night and said simply, "I believe."

• • •

Elisha Babcock, Jr., and Hampton L. Story believed in Coronado. In 1884 it was nothing more than an undeveloped, sandy peninsula on the western boundary of San Diego Bay, but Babcock and Story, two businessmen, envisioned a seaside resort of "magnificent splendor." Showing great ingenuity, the partners bought the entire

A full moon over the haunted Hotel del Coronado

peninsula, subdivided the land and then sold the individual lots to finance their grand resort hotel. They promised it would be the "talk of the western world," containing "a world of comfort, elegance and refined enjoyment." It was a promise that was duly fulfilled and, today, more than a century after its grand opening in 1888, the Hotel del Coronado remains one of the largest and most luxurious resort properties on the Pacific Coast.

The "Del" is famous for its white sand beaches, lush green lawns and serene ocean vistas. Its classic Queen Anne-style architecture and signature red-peaked roof have provided the setting for countless Hollywood films—including the 1959 classic *Some Like it Hot*—and it is believed to have been the visual inspiration for Frank Baum's Emerald City in *The Wizard of Oz.* Years later, in his novel *Bid Time Return,* author Richard Matheson set a romantic ghost story at the Hotel del Coronado. Certain elements of that fictional account echoed the facts of a real-life supernatural drama that began at the Del on November 24, 1892.

It was Thanksgiving Day when a beautiful young brunette checked into the grand resort under the name of "Lottie Anderson Bernard." She seemed unwell, the staff would later recall. One bellboy remembered her saying "that she had the neuralgia very bad." To others she reported that she had stomach cancer. But on the following Tuesday morning, when the dark-haired woman was found dead on a staircase leading to the ocean, it was not the result of any disease. The November 30, 1892, *San Diego Union* was one of the first to report the story:

A YOUNG WOMAN, SUFFERING FROM INCURABLE DISEASE, SUICIDES

She Wanders Out Into the Storm to Die—Desperate Act of a Guest of Hotel del Coronado—A Revolver the Chosen Weapon

Night before last an attractive, prepossessing and highly educated young woman came down from her room at Hotel del Coronado and between nine and ten o'clock stepped out upon the veranda facing the ocean, which was roaring at her very feet, lashed by the tempest that is sweeping over the whole coast. The lady was quietly and elegantly dressed in black and wore only a lace shawl over her head. Nothing more was seen of her until at 8:20 yesterday morning, when the assistant electrician of the hotel, passing by the shell walk at the end of the western terrace, saw the lady lying on the steps leading to the beach. She was dead.

A gun was found near the woman's body, and the coroner who attended to the case quickly ruled the cause of death to be "a pistol shot inflicted by her own hand with suicidal intent."

When the hotel management attempted to contact the woman's next of kin, they soon discovered that she had

Kate's forlorn spirit is often seen gazing out the window.

registered under an alias. Area newspapers ran articles and sketches that everyone hoped would assist in identifying "the beautiful stranger." Eventually the woman was identified as Kate Morgan of Iowa. When no one came forward to claim her body, she was buried in an unmarked grave.

For nearly 100 years, all that the staff at the Del Coronado knew about Kate Morgan was her name and the sad fact of her death. But in 1989 a San Francisco lawyer named Alan May became interested in the old story and began to search the archives for more information. Through painstaking research, he was able to piece together the journey that had led the young woman to her final days at the seaside resort.

May discovered that Morgan had been born Kate Farmer on September 23, 1865. The child's mother died shortly after her birth, and little Kate and her sister were raised primarily by their grandparents. Kate's father, George Farmer, was rarely involved with her upbringing. He did, however, teach her how to play poker.

By the time Kate was 20 years old, she was married to a handsome young gambler named Tom Morgan, whom she had met at one of her father's games. Soon the young couple was traveling back and forth across the country by train, making their living at high-stakes poker. Often Kate would pose as Tom's sister instead of his wife. This freed her to flirt seductively with the other card players, thereby distracting them and ensuring that her husband would walk away with the kitty.

The lifestyle seemed to suit them both, until Kate became pregnant in early 1889. The thought of a baby made the young woman yearn to settle down. Tom didn't share those yearnings, however, and the couple argued bitterly and went their separate ways. Kate ended up in San Francisco, where she found domestic work with a minister's family. When the baby was finally born, the minister and his wife adopted him as their own, and Kate went back to riding the rails with her itinerant husband.

It wasn't long, however, before Kate was pregnant again. Again, she and Tom argued over what to do. This time, Kate was more insistent that they should abandon their nomadic lifestyle and establish a real home. Tom was more insistent than ever that they should not. After another heated exchange, Tom sent Kate ahead to southern California, with promises that he would join her there eventually. And so it was that Kate Morgan checked into the Hotel del Coronado on that bleak Thanksgiving Day. She was suffering physically—either from complications of her pregnancy or, some believe, from a self-induced abortion. She was distraught, alone and, for some reason, felt the need to use an alias. Within five days, she would be dead.

This history, uncovered by Alan May's research, was all new information to the staff at the Del Coronado. All that the hotel's historians had ever known were the few sketchy facts surrounding the woman's death, as well as the rather unusual fact that since that day, the hotel had been haunted by a restless, unhappy spirit.

CERTIFICATE OF DEATH. ✓ 188

CORONER'S OFFICE,
CITY AND COUNTY OF SAN DIEGO.

San Diego, Cal., Dec 12 1892.

Name Mrs Kate Morgan

Aged 24 *years,* ~~*Male.*~~ *Female.*

Occupation — *Married.* ~~*Single. Widow. Widower.*~~

Place of Birth State or Country Iowa *Nationality* American

How long resident of this City or County, 4 days *years.*

Previous Residence, Los Angeles *Race* White

Place of Death, Coronado Beach

Date of Death, November 29th 1892

Date of Burial, December 13th 1892

Place of Interment, Mt Hope *Cemetery.*

Johnson Co *Undertaker.*

CORONER'S CERTIFICATE.

I, M. B. Kellar *Coroner, do hereby Certify, that having made all needed examination and inquiries on the body of above described decedent, I do hereby certify, that* Mrs Kate *came to* her *death in this* County *by* a pistol shot inflicted by her own hand with suicidal intent

M. B. Kellar
Coroner, City and County San Diego.
By H J Stetson Deputy Coroner

The last time Kate Morgan was seen alive, she was dressed in black with a lace shawl covering her dark hair. Not long after she was buried, guests and staff at the hotel began seeing a filmy image matching that description, gliding forlornly through the hallways. Sometimes her somber apparition would be seen staring out a window, as though she was waiting for someone. And strange, inexplicable things always happened in the room where she had stayed.

There were ghostly whispers—often heard but nearly impossible to interpret. There were disembodied footsteps, which could never be explained. The telephone would ring for no reason and the lights would flicker. Curtains would billow with mysterious breezes when the windows were tightly shut, and the television would turn on and off by itself. Guests who stayed in the room often mentioned that their cameras refused to work. Likewise, as the media became interested in the phenomena, most reporters found that Kate's ghost gave them trouble with their audio and video equipment. The radio personalities who had been attempting to set up their remote Halloween broadcast in the room had been forced to leave because not a single piece of their equipment would function. When they had finally all agreed that it would be best to return to the station, the television suddenly blasted on at full volume. Hitting the "power" button failed to turn it off, but it eventually shut down on its own, just as the engineer was about to pull the plug out of the wall.

The paranormal activity took place not only in the room that was Kate Morgan's but also in the room that once belonged to the chambermaid who would have attended to Kate. The maid in question vanished the day after Kate's funeral and was never seen again. There is no hard evidence that the women's lives were in any way intertwined or that the maid didn't simply move on to greener pastures—but some people have theorized that the two were connected in some dark way.

Theories, conjecture and wild fantasies seemed to flourish around the Hotel del Coronado's ghost story. One scribe noted that the story "suffered from being told too often." In fact, it was not the number of retellings, but the gross inaccuracies in them that were causing a problem. The media loved the idea of a ghost at the grand old resort, but treated it as light subject matter to play with as they pleased. They wove scandalous stories to explain the haunting, all of which were pure fiction. One of the wildest suggested that Kate was the pregnant mistress of Elisha Babcock, Jr. Another had her putting a gun to her head after catching her husband in the gaming room with another woman. It may have been this abundance of misinformation that caused the next twist in the Del's fascinating ghost story—for many believe that, in a supreme show of her spectral influence, Kate Morgan actually instigated an investigation into her own death.

Alan May, the lawyer who had become interested in Kate's story in 1989, found that his interest quickly evolved into an obsession. For a year he used his expertise to uncover and examine every document associated with the woman's life and death. He frequently stayed at the Del, where he felt that Kate's spirit directed him in the course of his investigation. At the end of it all, he determined two amazing facts. The first was that Kate's death was the result of murder, not suicide. The .38 caliber bullet in her head didn't match the .44 caliber gun that had been found near her hand, and the entrance wound was inconsistent with a self-inflicted gunshot. May speculated that Tom Morgan, unwilling to be burdened with a pregnant partner, had followed Kate to the Del and killed her. May's second revelation was that Kate's baby, adopted by the San Francisco minister in 1889, had been Alan Mayer May—Alan May's own grandfather. Alan May quickly realized that the tragic and lovely Kate Morgan had been his own great-grandmother and began to understand why he had been "chosen" to unravel the mystery. It was an astounding discovery, but not the last in this story of extraordinary coincidences.

During the summer of 1990, a couple named Bev and Gerry Rush checked into the Hotel del Coronado for a weekend getaway. During their first night's stay, Gerry Rush was awakened in the wee hours of the morning by the sound of a woman crying inconsolably. It seemed to Rush that the sound was coming from the hallway, so he pulled on a pair of shorts and opened the door to investigate. There, crouched on the floor, was a young woman wearing an old-fashioned maid's uniform. When Gerry Rush asked her what was the matter, she sobbed, "I was murdered!"

By the next morning, the incident had taken on a dream-like quality. Rush was about to write it off to the previous evening's cocktails when a crumpled piece of clothing by the hotel room door caught his attention. He picked the item up and saw that it was the pair of shorts he had put on before he had walked out in the hall and discovered the weeping maid.

Later that day, Rush was still disturbed and confused about what had actually taken place. He mentioned his strange experience to the bellman who had escorted the

Rushes to their room and was asked, "Haven't you heard about our ghost?" When Gerry Rush shook his head, the bellman suggested that he visit the gift shop, which carried a book about the haunting.

Gerry Rush did just that. As he paid for his purchase, he noticed that the author of the book *Kate Morgan, Who Are You?* (Elk Publishing, 1989) was Alan M. May. Gerry Rush quickly checked the author's photo and confirmed that it was a man he remembered best as Sergeant May from Vietnam. Sergeant May had served in the same special unit as Gerry Rush and had once saved his life. As he settled down to read his new book, Rush resolved to get back in touch with his old army buddy.

By the end of the book, Gerry Rush's desire to reconnect with Alan May had become urgent. After reading May's account of the story, he was convinced that he had met the specter of the maid who had disappeared after Kate Morgan's funeral. He was equally certain that the maid had materialized specifically for him—knowing that he had a connection to May and would be sure to pass on the information. After decades of attempting to gain attention through her poltergeist antics, the maid found a way to ensure that her story would also finally be told.

And finally it was. An expanded and revised edition of Alan May's book, entitled *The Legend of Kate Morgan: The Search for the Ghost of the Hotel del Coronado,* was published soon after. Along with Kate's poignant story, it contained an addendum that speculated that the maid had been killed after witnessing Kate's murder. It also contained the sad information that Alan May himself had passed away in 1992—exactly one century after the murder of his great-grandmother, Kate Morgan. Fortunately, in his final years May had had enough time to unravel Kate's mystery, tell her story and place a proper marker on her grave.

And yet, the haunting continues.

Staff at the Del still hear frequent stories of unusual things that happen to guests in the two haunted rooms—so it would seem that the spirits of Kate Morgan and the maid are unwilling to relinquish their beautiful seaside haunt, although their stories have now been told.

Given the spectacular setting, no one can blame them. Any discriminating person—dead or alive—would be proud to call the luxurious Hotel del Coronado home.

The Hotel Queen Mary

Once she was the most famous ocean liner in the world, renowned for her size, her speed and her atmosphere of unparalleled luxury. For 14 years she held the world's record for the fastest crossing of the Atlantic Ocean. She transported royalty, movie stars, dignitaries and heads of state, all of whom believed that the only "civilized" way to travel was aboard RMS *Queen Mary*.

In 1967 the *Queen Mary* stopped sailing—but she seemed unwilling to stop setting records. Today, as she sits in dry-dock in Long Beach, California, the *Queen Mary* is notable partly because she is thought to be the most haunted hotel in the world.

Every year guests and staff write endless reports about ghostly sightings and various paranormal phenomena. The well-known psychic Peter James, once commissioned to study the paranormal activity on board, concluded that more than 600 spirits regarded the great ship to be their afterlife home. Given all this psychic activity, it seems appropriate that when the *Queen Mary* was launched, it was with a psychic prediction:

> RMS *Queen Mary,* launched today, will know her greatest fame and popularity when she never sails another mile and never carries another paying passenger.

Those were the words of Lady Mabel Fortescue-Harrison, an English astrologer and one of an estimated 200,000 people gathered to see the *Queen Mary* launched from Clydebank, Scotland, on a cold September day in 1934. It was a prophecy destined to come true—but before it could come true, the *Queen* would spend more than 30 eventful years at sea.

The Cunard Line designed the *Queen Mary* to be outstanding in both opulence and sheer size. The ship ran more than 1000 feet from bow to stern, weighed 81,237 gross tons and was outfitted with the most luxurious appointments. But she was more than just a floating palace. Four steam turbines, generating 40,000 horsepower each, ensured that the *Queen* was also one of the fastest ships of her day.

Her legendary size and speed were likely why the *Queen Mary* was immediately conscripted into service when England declared war with Germany. Overnight, the ship was stripped of her magnificence, outfitted with army bunks and camouflaged in a dull shade of ocean-gray paint. Then, nicknamed "The Gray Ghost," the ship began

The *Queen Mary*, now permanently docked in Long Beach, California

her military career as a massive troop transport.

The *Queen Mary* was an invaluable addition to the British war effort. She was astonishingly fast, nearly invisible in her camouflage and capable of outmaneuvering any German warship. She was well equipped to transport 5000 soldiers at a time and, at the height of the hostilities, carried a record 16,683. Perhaps the greatest indicator of her worth to the Allies was that Hitler made a standing offer of $250,000 and Germany's highest military honor to any captain who could sink her. The *Queen Mary* seemed untouchable, however, and by the end of World War II, she had carried more than 800,000 troops and played some part in every major Allied campaign.

After delivering the North American troops home (along with thousands of British war brides and their babies), the *Queen Mary* reclaimed her position as one of the world's most elegant modes of travel. For 20 more years, she transported the rich and the famous on their ocean voyages. Then, in 1967, after 1001 transatlantic crossings, the *Queen* dropped anchor for the last time. She was permanently docked at Long Beach, California, and, from that day forward, would never "[sail] another mile" or "[carry] another paying passenger." As the massive ship underwent the conversion into a hotel and attraction, Lady Mabel Fortescue-Harrison's prophecy began to come true. The *Queen Mary* was about to enter the era of her greatest fame.

As the ship underwent her unprecedented three-year renovation, strange stories began to emerge. Some members of the construction crew working deep in the ship's hull spoke hesitantly of the unusual noises and voices they heard there. Security guards left alone in the dark, silent ship at night reported that their dogs refused to patrol certain places on board. The various accounts accumulated and eventually it became apparent that when the powerfully fast *Queen Mary* had finally stopped moving, she had allowed her past to catch up with her.

The *Queen*'s ghost stories were so convincing because nearly identical experiences were reported by different witnesses on different occasions, sometimes years apart. From such numerous objective reports, staff at the *Queen Mary* have been able to identify several specific phantoms aboard the ship.

One of the best known is John Pedder, "The Shaft Alley Specter." ("Shaft Alley" is an area next to the engine room, so named because it houses propeller shafts.) Pedder was killed on July 10, 1966, during a routine drill. The 18-year-old either overestimated the time he had to slip through a closing water-tight door, or he was playing a deadly game of "chicken" with a fellow employee. He was found crushed to death by "Door 13" in the engine room. His spirit has been seen in the area many times since then.

Nancy Wazny, a former tour guide and security officer with the *Queen Mary*, reported a typical encounter with John Pedder. She was locking up the engine room exhibit one night when she sensed that someone was standing behind her. She turned around, expecting to see a person who had become separated from a tour group. But the bearded young man she saw didn't look the part of a tourist. He was clad in dirty, dark-blue coveralls, had "grossly white" skin and a complete lack of facial expression. Before Wazny could think of what to do, the apparition vanished before her eyes.

Another familiar spirit aboard the *Queen Mary* is the ghost of Senior Second Officer William Eric Stark. Stark has been seen wandering about the ship since 1949 when, like John Pedder, he met an untimely, accidental death. Unlike Pedder, Stark did not die quickly. He suffered for four long days after taking a large drink of lime juice laced with poisonous carbon tetrachloride, which he had mistaken for gin.

If Stark's spirit is in search of a drinking partner of similar rank, he is in luck. There is another spectral officer aboard the ship. Many witnesses have come forward over the years to report seeing a man wearing an immaculate dress uniform and walking about on deck. No one ever mistakes this particular apparition for a live human being, for although the man's image is very distinct, it is decidedly transparent.

The *Queen Mary* is haunted by more than her past personnel, however. During her years as a luxury liner, more than two million passengers enjoyed her elegant accommodations. Many, it would seem, have decided to extend their stays indefinitely. Among the best known of these ghostly guests are the spectral swimmers and the beautiful lady in white.

The "lady in white"—a lovely woman dressed in a backless, formal gown—is frequently seen in a room that was once the first-class lounge (it is now the Queen's Salon). Perhaps some celebrant from a party long ago, she dances alone in the shadows. According to one account related by present-day staff,

> One unsuspecting little girl pointed out to the tour guide "the woman in white." The tour guide looked over and saw nothing; however, the little girl described the woman in detail. Still, the guide saw nothing and continued with the tour. The child continued to repeat her observation, not knowing that she was just one in a long list of those who had seen this mysterious woman.

The spectral swimmers are a number of ghosts, apparently from different eras, who haunt the area around the eye-catching, art-deco swimming pool. Tour guides, security personnel and guests have seen fleeting images of women in old-fashioned bathing suits. One guide reported seeing a diver from another era appear to her in "black and white." Splashing noises have often been heard as well. One employee reported investigating the pool area when he heard the sound and finding a trail of wet footprints that ended suddenly, as though the feet making them had vanished. This phenomenon is particularly interesting because the pool has been kept empty and unused for a number of years. It is also protected by a highly sensitive alarm system, which its otherworldly users never seem to trigger.

Although the common areas seem to be the most dramatically haunted, several staterooms have seen their share of mysterious occurrences over the years. Smoke from Winston Churchill's famous cigars has been detected in the stateroom he often occupied. Other rooms are known for such curiosities as lights that turn on by themselves in the middle of the night and unseen hands that reposition luggage and other personal effects. One particular room—which once belonged to a purser who was murdered during a robbery—is so filled with poltergeist activity that it is no longer rented out. People who stayed in it were forced to endure shaking beds, rattling drawers, flying objects and invisible clutching hands.

The murder of the purser is but one in a long list of casualties that took place aboard the *Queen Mary.* The first was a fatal accident that took place during her construction. Since then, there have been at least 55 documented deaths, ranging from natural causes to suicide. Without a doubt, though, many other violent, emotionally charged deaths took place during the ship's wartime service.

During the war, the *Queen Mary* often carried two, or even three, times the number of people she could accommodate in relative comfort. The troops would sleep in shifts so that as many as three men could use the same bunk. Many passengers were prisoners of war, forced to occupy the stifling space well below deck. There were deaths resulting from battle injuries, heat exhaustion and the violence that often erupted in the intolerable conditions.

There is a record of one such brawl in 1943. The men were apparently unhappy with the quality of the food and had swarmed into the galley to confront the cook. Tempers flared and a huge riot ensued. The ship's captain feared a general mutiny and placed a call for assistance. If help ever did arrive, though, it was too late for the cook. During the melee, he was shoved into a heated oven. He died from the resulting burns, and his spirit remains in that kitchen today. He keeps busy by rattling plates, moving utensils around and occasionally switching the lights on and off.

Without a doubt, however, the single most tragic event in the *Queen Mary*'s history was the sinking of HMS *Curacoa* in the early 1940s. The two ships were sailing together, with the anti-aircraft cruiser acting as a protective escort. The *Queen Mary*'s standard wartime practice was to maintain a zigzag pattern. At some point a navigational error was made, and the huge ship collided with her smaller escort at high speed. The *Curacoa* was sliced in two, and her 439 crewmen spilled out into the freezing waters of the North Atlantic. Of those men, 338 died as they watched the mighty *Queen Mary* sail away. The ship was carrying 10,000 troops on that voyage and was under strict orders not to stop for any reason.

The damage sustained to the *Queen Mary*'s bow on that day was temporarily mended with a 70-ton patch of cement. Years later, however, when the ship was retired from service, it became apparent that there were deeper, psychic scars, which could not be so easily covered up.

John Smith, who was the *Queen*'s chief engineer at that time, may have been the first to realize how the trauma had imprinted itself upon the ship's atmosphere. Frequently he would hear the sound of water rushing into the area that had been damaged in the tragic accident. Smith knew his ship inside and out, and he conducted extensive searches in an effort to locate the source of the sound. In the end, however, he could find no reasonable explanation. He had to conclude that he was hearing a ghostly echo of the accident.

Many of the *Queen Mary*'s staff have heard those sounds—and others—emanating from what was once the damaged part of the hull. The ship's staff reported that, on one occasion, those eerie noises were captured for all to hear. According to a hotel news release,

> Forty years [after the accident], a television crew left their audio recorder running overnight in the exact location where the two ships collided. As the tape played back the next day, incredible sounds of pounding could be heard. Others have claimed to have heard voices and blood-curdling noises from the same area.

Mysterious sounds and voices have always been a large part of the paranormal phenomena aboard the *Queen Mary*. Tom Hennessy, a columnist for the *Long Beach Press-Telegram*, once spent a night in various locations on the haunted ship. While in "Shaft Alley," he was party to a spectral conversation, which he described in his March 6, 1983, column:

> Initially, it sounded like two or three men talking at once. But it trailed off into a single voice, so distinct that I made out—or thought I made out—the end of a sentence: "...turning the lights off."

Later, as Hennessy spoke to security staff, he theorized that the voices might have been carried via an air duct from another part of the ship.

"No way," the guard told him. "In fact, about the time you were up there, the nearest person to you was a security officer who was two decks away."

In other areas of the ship, particularly the nurseries, disembodied children's voices are the norm. Laughter and the cheerful sounds of play are most often heard—but there are melancholy exceptions. In the original third-class children's playroom, where a toddler died in the late 1940s, many people have heard a child crying. There have also been reports of an infant wailing. It is believed to be the spirit of young Leigh Travers Smith, who died aboard the *Queen Mary* only a few hours after his birth. The most fascinating child entity on the ship, however, is very likely a little girl known as "Jackie." When psychic Peter James began his investigation into the *Queen Mary*'s haunting, he met Jackie and found that he was easily able to communicate with her. The more the child spoke to James, the more clear her voice became. The little spirit's presence was so strong that, amazingly, her words eventually became audible for all to hear. The rare phenomenon was captured on tape and witnessed by a large number of people.

Peter James' extensive research led him to believe that there were hundreds of phantoms aboard the *Queen Mary* and that the first-class pool's dressing room contained a "vortex"—which he described as a doorway between dimensions. Even without such a portal of entry, though, it would be easy to understand why the ship is so very haunted. She's seen decades of drama, numerous deaths and much joy and contentment. It is conceivable that, while many of the spirits on board remain trapped because of their violent or untimely ends, many others were drawn to the ship following their deaths because it is the place where they spent the happiest times of their lives.

Today, the *Queen Mary* is a first-rate hotel, the crown jewel of the Queen Mary Seaport attraction and can boast inclusion in the National Register of Historic Places. Add to the list that she is considered one of the most haunted locations in the world, and it's plain to see that Lady Mabel Fortescue-Harrison was right. Though she will never "[sail] another mile or [carry] another paying passenger," the haunted RMS *Queen Mary* surely knows her greatest fame today.

Vineyard House

The historic town of Coloma, in El Dorado County, is the heart of California's "gold country." It is the place where, in 1848, a lumber mill foreman named James Marshall discovered the glittering nugget that eventually brought tens of thousands of prospectors rushing to the state. It was a wild time, marked by violence, big dreams, bitter disappointment and greed. The exciting and dangerous atmosphere may have eventually created a mother lode of a different sort: a rich, supernatural vein of ghosts.

There may be no better example of such historically induced haunting than Coloma's famous Vineyard House. It was built during the boom years as a hotel and has only recently become a private residence. At last report, all paranormal activity had calmed, but for more than a century, a succession of owners, employees and hotel guests experienced countless inexplicable events. To those who knew the history of the large, Victorian-style building, the strange happenings came as no surprise. Most felt that any place that had seen so much drama and tragedy was bound to be filled with restless spirits.

Vineyard House was built in 1878 by Robert and Louise Chalmers. They were a well-respected, prosperous couple who made their fortune not by panning for gold but by providing for the huge population of those who did. They had their vineyards and an award-winning winery. Robert enjoyed a moderately successful political career, serving one term as a state senator. With the grand opening of Vineyard House on April 4, 1879, the Chalmers became the charming proprietors of a fine hotel that was the scene of every significant social event in the area.

Success was relatively short-lived, though. Robert Chalmers designed Vineyard House to be a family business, a happy home and an enduring symbol of his status in the community. Instead, it became the scene of his frightening descent into madness.

Not long after Vineyard House opened, Louise began to notice peculiar changes in her husband's behavior. His memory had become unreliable, and he often did or said strange things. He whispered to himself incessantly, showed signs of extreme paranoia and, on occasion, would wander into the cemetery across the road to lie in a freshly dug grave with his arms crossed over his chest. As time went on, Robert's condition grew more frightening. He began to throw frequent temper tantrums and eventually his angry outbursts were accompanied by violent threats. It is not entirely clear whether Louise was worried about Robert's own safety (her first husband had died by his own hand) or whether she was concerned for herself and her children, but she eventually had Robert confined to the cellar of the house. There, he declined rapidly until he eventually refused all meals, certain that his wife was attempting to poison him. Robert Chalmers died in 1881. He was buried across the road from Vineyard House, in Pioneer Cemetery, where he had tried so many of the graves out for size.

Robert's death contributed to a long line of hardships for Louise. Her grape vines, attacked by a blight, soon withered and died. A son from Robert Chalmers' first marriage filed a civil suit, claiming a share of his father's estate. The money was going out faster than it was coming in, and the creditors began to loom. Eventually a bank that held a large mortgage on the property foreclosed. Louise was permitted to stay in Vineyard House but had to pay rent. That in itself presented a challenge for the financially strapped widow—but it was a challenge Louise met with admirable creativity.

First she reduced the price of the rooms to ensure that they would be continually occupied. It lowered the standard of the hotel to that of a rooming house but guaranteed an income. Second she rented out her late husband's dungeon-like cell for use as the town's auxiliary jail. Many criminals did their time in Louise Chalmers' cellar—and at least two men spent their final hours there. Both were convicted murderers who were hanged at a gallows which, for the sake of convenience, had been constructed right on Louise's front lawn.

In 1913 Louise Chalmers died. She was buried in Pioneer Cemetery alongside Robert. Soon after, their proud, Victorian mansion, which had once been the social epicenter of Coloma, began to inch its way into a state of disrepair. Another phase of Vineyard House's strange, interesting history was about to begin.

For many years, owners came and went with regularity. Sometimes as they left, they would mention the inexplicable noises and discomforting experiences that had encouraged them to sell the property. Sometimes they just moved on. With increasing frequency, tenants moved out too, complaining of the sounds of rattling chains, clanging metal, breathy whispers and disembodied footsteps in the dark corridors. One boarder ran from the building in the middle of the night, never to return. He refused to say exactly what it was that had inspired his unceremonious departure.

In 1956 there was a renovation. The cellar jail was converted into a cozy bar, and the upstairs rooms were refurbished. Vineyard House was reopened as a respectable restaurant and inn, but many say that the ghosts stayed on. In the decades that followed, guests and employees alike experienced things that could not be explained, except to say that Robert, Louise and a number of their spectral friends considered themselves to be in permanent residence.

Over the years, the collection of strange stories grew. Many people who had spent time in Vineyard House reported that small, unsettling events took place regularly. It was said that doorknobs would turn as though touched by an invisible hand and that footsteps were often clearly heard on the stairs leading to the cellar bar, although no one could be seen descending. Some guests would securely lock the doors to their rooms at night, then awaken in the morning to find them standing ajar. It was reported that on one occasion a maid, who was alone in the hotel, discovered turned-back covers and the impression of a body on the sheets of a bed she had just freshly made up. A bartender and a customer once watched in disbelief as two glasses trembled with some unseen force and then slid across the bar. And in 1987, a husband and wife grabbed their bags and raced off in the middle of the night. They did not stop until they reached the sheriff's office in Placerville, where they reported that they had clearly heard a murder take place in Vineyard House, in the room next to theirs. The police investigated and found nothing amiss. Some time later, however, a psychically sensitive woman (who knew nothing of this story) told the owners that when she walked into the room in question, she was overwhelmed by negative emotions.

Several dramatic tales involved actual apparitions. One couple was awakened from a sound sleep by a group of late-night revelers. The voices and laughter grew louder as the inconsiderate party tromped up the stairs. The couple threw open the door to their room, intending to confront the group. The instant they saw the noisy bunch, however, their annoyance turned to astonishment. There, at the top of the stairs, stood three gentlemen dressed in Victorian attire. They regarded the startled guests for a moment before their images slowly faded away.

It is not surprising that one of the most recognizable specters at Vineyard House is said to be Robert Chalmers himself. Over the years, several guests claimed to see the somber-looking, bearded man in either the restaurant or the cellar bar. Could it simply have been someone matching his description? It's unlikely, as this particular "patron" was known to vanish through a solid brick wall.

It was often said that Robert would pound on the walls or appear to harass people whose behavior displeased him. Supporting that claim is a story told by one Coloma resident who once took his girlfriend upstairs to view one of Vineyard House's redecorated rooms. When the girlfriend wasn't looking, the man turned out the light. It was a practical joke meant to startle the girl. When the bedsprings creaked, he thought that the prank had failed and that his girlfriend had calmly sat down to wait for the light to come back on. When he flipped the switch on, however, he discovered that his girlfriend was still standing beside him. Sitting on the bed was a stern-looking Robert Chalmers, who glared at the unnerved man for several seconds before he appeared to dissolve.

Legend has it that Louise's ghost has been seen too—although at least one of those stories places her not at the hotel, but at the cemetery across the road where she is buried. Still, many believed that Louise had a spectral hand in managing Vineyard House long after her death. In *Gold Rush Ghosts* (Borderland Sciences Research Foundation, 1990), authors Nancy Bradley and Vincent Gaddis recounted the frustrating and mysterious problems encountered by one group of owners when they undertook a massive renovation of the building in 1975.

One of the owners, Gary Herrera, was quoted as saying "I would painstakingly choose colors and fabrics, ordering vibrant shades for bedspreads, curtains, wallpaper, paint and accessories. [But] my order would arrive in completely contrasting shades..."

Herrera was utterly confused until he found an old scrapbook documenting the early days of Vineyard

House. As he flipped through the pages, he realized that the countless "incorrect" shipments had perfectly matched the house's original decor. It seemed that there was some mysterious force unwilling to see the hotel undergo too dramatic a transformation.

It has now been a few years since Vineyard House has been open to the public as a hotel. Locals report that things are quiet there now—a situation that no doubt pleases the current residents. As for those people who delight in a good haunting, there are decades' worth of stories about Vineyard House to retell and to analyze. For decades to come, those tales will serve to entertain, intrigue and remind us that, among believers, California's famous "gold country" might one day also be known as "ghost country."

Hollywood Roosevelt Hotel

It is nearly noon, and a well-dressed woman hurries through the halls of the luxurious Hollywood Roosevelt Hotel on her way to the dining room to meet a companion for lunch. A tall mirror with a heavy, dark frame stands against one wall, and the woman pauses before it for a quick, final appraisal of her appearance. Suddenly she gasps and jumps back from the mirror but not because she has found fault with her own looks… Although she is entirely alone in the hallway, the face that gazes out of the mirror at her is not her own…

• • •

It is a Monday morning, and Billy from Engineering is working on the third floor of the hotel. As he walks through the halls he notices a lone man who is looking first one way and then the other, as though he is lost. Billy calls out, asking if he can be of assistance. The man does not reply. Billy walks down the hall toward the man and asks again. Still he receives no answer. Then, when Billy is no more than three feet away from him, the apparently lost man turns and walks through the fire exit. He doesn't open the door—he just walks *through* it. Billy tries to follow, but finds that for several seconds he is unable to move.

• • •

The famed psychic Peter James is exploring the basement of the historic hotel with his assistant, a camera operator and two other people. The group is walking through one particularly dark, deserted area when James suddenly stops them.

"Wait!" he says. "There is someone here—right over here!"

The Hollywood Roosevelt Hotel, home to stars both dead and alive

The group walks quietly to a back corner, where a number of heavy bedspreads have been draped over a high rod. James shushes his companions and points to the spreads. He begins to talk to the female spirit whom he senses there. As he speaks, the onlookers are amazed to see one bedspread in the center of all of the others begin to move. It sways gently at first, then undulates with more force as Peter James asks the spirit to tell him her name and explain why she is there. Then, quite suddenly, the movement stops. James calls out to the spirit, but she is gone.

The frustrated psychic steps in front of the hanging bedspread, where he had seen the ghostly woman.

"Come here. Feel this," he says to his companions.

Each of them, in turn, steps into the small space which the spirit had occupied. The air there is frigid.

"That shaft of cold air was caused by her exit," Peter James explains.

• • •

The Hollywood Roosevelt Hotel first opened its doors

in 1927. It was glamorous and luxurious, designed to serve the elite members of the town's dazzling film industry. The hotel, named after Theodore Roosevelt, succeeded in capturing the excitement and romance of Hollywood's golden era. It quickly became known as "The Home of the Stars" and would eventually become a cherished Hollywood landmark.

History was often written within the Roosevelt's elegant walls. On May 16, 1929, the first-ever Academy Awards presentation (then called the Merit Awards) was held in the hotel's Blossom Ballroom. And from 1927 through 1935, every meeting of the Motion Pictures Academy of Arts and Sciences took place in the hotel library—an area now called the "Academy Room." Shirley Temple learned to do her famous staircase dance on the steps leading from the lobby to the mezzanine. During Prohibition Errol Flynn was said to have mixed his notorious gin cocktails in the back of the hotel barbershop. Clark Gable and Carol Lombard frequently sequestered themselves in one of the luxuriously appointed suites for a romantic getaway. And, in the Cinegrill Lounge, Ernest Hemingway, F. Scott Fitzgerald and Salvador Dali would meet to listen to the latest jazz acts.

In those early, glittering days the Hollywood Roosevelt hosted many of the most famous names in the movies—as well as a few who had not quite yet achieved fame. Mary Martin's first paying job as a singer was in the Cinegrill, and a young David Niven was once permitted to stay in a tiny room in the hotel's staff quarters when he was unemployed, penniless and fresh on the Hollywood scene.

There were flesh-and-blood stars living lavishly inside the hotel and pink granite stars lying outside the front door, immortalizing movie greats on the legendary "Walk of Fame." It was magnificent and magical. But, like Hollywood's golden era, the Roosevelt's heyday could not last forever. Years passed and the hotel faded.

Fortunately, there were those who were not willing to see such an important piece of Hollywood's history lost to the ravages of time. In 1984 a group of investors purchased the Hollywood Roosevelt Hotel. They closed its doors and proceeded to spend two years and 35 million dollars restoring "The Home of the Stars" to its original grandeur.

The official reopening gala, attended by more than 1500 dignitaries and film industry notables, took place on March 7, 1986. By that time, the hand-painted ceilings and Spanish wrought-iron grill work had been painstakingly refurbished. More than 300 rooms and luxury suites had been returned to a state of splendor. The hotel was once again beautiful, expertly staffed and prepared to host magnificent premiere parties, celebrity receptions and gala events of all kinds. Admirers were reminded of the glorious past—the days when the Hollywood Roosevelt Hotel had been a major player in the city. As it turned out, however, the renovation had stirred up more than just nostalgia. That had become keenly evident nearly three months earlier, as staff had hurriedly prepared to open the hotel in a limited capacity. During that hectic time, in December 1985, the first of many strange and dramatic occurrences took place.

Alan Russell's job was to act as a personal assistant to the general manager—but on one particular day, two weeks prior to the opening, he was sweeping the floor. It was not just any floor, however; it was the floor of the

Blossom Ballroom, where the Academy Awards had long ago been presented. Russell, who was also an actor, viewed the chore as an opportunity to "commune with the spirits" of the stars. Happily he imagined his own award acceptance speech as he cleaned the floor in preparation for the carpet that was about to be laid.

As Alan Russell worked from one end of the ballroom to the other, he noticed that one small area seemed to be cooler than the rest of the room. At first, he paid little attention to the dip in temperature. After passing through the spot several times, however, he became curious. There were no open doors or windows that could have allowed a draft, there were no trap doors in the floor, and the air conditioners had not yet been connected. Eventually, Russell called a fellow employee into the room to help him investigate. Neither man could find a reason why the column of air, approximately 30 inches in diameter, was a full 10 degrees cooler than the rest of the room.

On that same day, a woman named Suzanne Leonard was startled while she dusted a tall, framed mirror in the general manager's office. Though Leonard was alone in the room, she saw the image of a lovely, young, blonde woman reflected in the glass as she polished it. Thinking that she had company, Leonard turned to greet the woman. She found no one standing behind her. That unnerved Leonard a little, but she dutifully turned back to her cleaning chore. When she saw that the reflection of the beautiful blonde was still visible in the mirror, though, she was more than unnerved. She went searching for the manager and asked him about the mirror. He informed Suzanne Leonard that it had once belonged to Marilyn Monroe and that it had been removed from the star's

This mirror once belonged to Marilyn Monroe and is said to be haunted by her image.

favorite pool-side suite.

The hotel maids were also busy during that time. There were hundreds upon hundreds of beds to make up, carpets to be vacuumed, furniture to be dusted and towels to be stocked in every room. One day, as a maid carrying towels approached room 928, she felt a cool breeze travel over her arms. That alone might have been forgotten had the door not slammed shut behind the woman after she walked into the room. It seemed impossible—the room doors were all on compression hinges and were, therefore, incapable of slamming. The woman was a bit shaken but went ahead and stocked the room with towels. Moments later, when she walked out of the room, she felt a cold form brush past her in the hallway.

If the woman was hoping to find someone who could corroborate her story, she did not have to wait long. Later the same day, two other ninth-floor maids emphatically declared that they would *not* be entering room 928 again, because "there was something strange there."

These dramatic, seemingly paranormal incidents were among the first to be reported at the Hollywood Roosevelt Hotel. But they would be far from the last. Before long, the director of security began to maintain a log of such strange happenings. The notebook rapidly filled up with reports from both staff and guests.

Prior to the grand reopening, the hotel was open, but not all floors were completed and in use. One night, the lobby switchboard received a call from a room that was unfinished, unoccupied and, most significantly, had no telephone. On another occasion, the assistant director of housekeeping, Daniel Cichon, turned off all the lights and locked the door of a room he had finished inspecting. When he returned moments later, the lights were on once more. Cichon, the only person holding a key to that room, was understandably mystified. A lobby maid named Rachel might have told Cichon to consider himself lucky. The phantom that she encountered had the nerve to push her into a supply closet.

The truth was, the ghosts of the Hollywood Roosevelt Hotel seemed to delight in creating little challenges for the staff as they went about their duties. A sales coordinator named Karen Bookholt once had to work alone in her office as she tried to block out the distraction of a typewriter that was typing by itself. Another employee named Steve Fava had his nerves similarly tested in the summer of 1988, as he went from floor to floor refilling the soda machines.

Each time Fava began, he placed the clipboard that held his paperwork on top of the soda machine. Each time he finished stocking the cans, the clipboard had moved to a different, unlikely location—*inside* the ice machine, which sat an arm's length away. On the first floor, Fava tried to think of a logical explanation for the clipboard's movement. By the tenth floor, he was pale with fright.

"Don't ever make me do that again!" he told the general manager when he had finished the assignment.

Steve Fava's feelings were understandable. Still, he might have taken a moment to feel grateful that he worked in the purchasing department and not for hotel security. It was those employees who suffered most at the hands of the Roosevelt's unseen guests—for it was usually someone from security who would be dispatched to solve the impossible problems created by the ghosts.

The hotel's security staff made countless trips to vacant rooms because of complaints about the "noisy" guests staying in them. They spent many unsuccessful hours searching the hallways for reported late-night revelers. In October 1989, security guards made trip after trip to room 1221 to put the telephone back on the hook. Someone or something in that room kept trying to contact the switchboard—which was odd, because the room was unoccupied...

During the same period, several new security personnel were hired. After a couple of weeks on the job, one new guard mentioned to a fellow employee that, night after night, he could not shake the eerie feeling that he was being watched. It must have been a creepy sensation, but the guard's invisibly monitored patrol was still light duty compared to a fellow security guard's assignment. That man had been sent out with instructions to quiet a cabana room full of rowdy, phantom children.

Of course not all the spectral children who inhabit the Hollywood Roosevelt have been apt to misbehave. One little girl—thought by one psychic to be named Carol or Caroline—is actually quite charming. A hotel employee named Rachael encountered her in the nearly deserted lobby very early one morning, as she arrived for her shift.

"She was so cute, skipping around the fountain and singing," Rachael recalled. The child looked to be about five years old. She was wearing blue jeans with a pink jacket and had her light brown hair pulled back in a ponytail. She was following a man who was walking across the lobby toward the front desk. But when Rachael asked the man if the little girl was his daughter, he looked confused.

"No, I don't have any children," he said.

Rachael must have immediately wondered why such a young child was out alone at such an early hour. She turned to speak to the little girl—and, to her surprise, saw that she was gone. In a matter of two or three seconds, in a large, open area, the child had simply vanished.

The little girl is only one of many apparitions that have been seen in the hotel. A night desk clerk named Troy Robertson was badly shocked one night when a man walked past the table where he was counting his receipts. That the man was a ghost was fairly obvious—for he was lacking a face. Robertson was understandably upset by the incident. While he remains certain of what he saw that night, he generally avoids discussing it.

In December 1990, a couple who had just attended a Christmas party at the Hollywood Roosevelt met another of the hotel's spectral guests. The man and woman had followed the sound of piano music onto the balcony that overlooks the Blossom Ballroom. A man in a white suit stood near the piano there. The couple approached the man and spoke to him but received no response. Perhaps thinking that the man hadn't heard them, the couple moved a few steps closer. Apparently they were *too* close for the comfort of the man in the white suit—for he vanished right before the astonished couple's eyes.

It is interesting to note that it was the following Monday morning when Billy from Engineering witnessed the "lost man" walking through the closed fire escape door. Over the years, many people have wondered if these were two sightings of the same ghost—for Billy described the man he saw as wearing "old shoes and a white suit."

Of course the most recognizable face to ever appear posthumously at the Hollywood Roosevelt Hotel is the beautiful blonde image that gazes out of Marilyn Monroe's mirror. (The mirror now sits in a public area of the hotel, so that guests may have the opportunity to witness the phenomenon.) But it is widely known that Marilyn is not the only famous phantom on the permanent guest list. Psychics have sensed the "presences" of numerous well-known performers, including Carmen Miranda, Errol Flynn, Betty Grable, Gypsy Rose Lee, Humphrey Bogart, Ethel Merman, Charles Laughton, Edward Arnold and others. Marilyn has also been sensed in the Tropicana Bar, which is beside the pool where she modeled for her first advertisement (suntan lotion) and just below the cabana room where she often stayed. Many of these personalities have been described by psychics as "impressions," as though during their lifetimes, they left an imprint of sorts on the atmosphere of the hotel. By contrast, there is one Hollywood star who is, without a doubt, spending a very active afterlife at the Roosevelt.

Montgomery Clift spent three months in room 928 of the Hollywood Roosevelt while he was filming *From Here to Eternity*. He was said to pace up and down the hall outside his room while he rehearsed his lines and blew a bugle. These loud, eccentric habits may have made Clift a less-than-model guest, but they didn't prevent him from staying for as long as he wanted. Now it seems that the spirit of the handsome actor is intent upon occupying that room "to eternity." The maids who experienced strange sensations, icy chills and slamming doors in room 928 prior to the reopening may have been the first to know.

Hotel guests in the neighboring room will often complain about the noise on the other side of the wall, even when room 928 is vacant. Tinny, old-fashioned bugle music is sometimes heard in the vicinity. And Clift's spirit has been known to get quite up close and personal with guests who stay in "his" room. One woman was lying on her side in bed, reading, when she distinctly felt a pat on the shoulder. She turned to see what it was that her husband wanted—and saw that he was still fast asleep in the *other* bed. The woman had just received a "good-night pat" from Monty Clift.

Naturally, this combination of ghostly mysteries and celebrity names has proven irresistible to the media. Since the reopening, numerous television crews have descended upon the Hollywood Roosevelt, hoping to capture some of the anomalous activity on video. The spirits seem to enjoy the attention, although they've *not* been terribly cooperative.

In October 1989, a television crew experienced one problem after another as they tried to shoot a Halloween special at the hotel. When they were in the Blossom Ballroom, the cold spot distorted their audio equipment. When they tried to get a shot of Marilyn's mirror, a false fire alarm forced them to abandon the scene. And when the crew set up their equipment outside room 928, the house lights went out *twice*, the sound equipment failed, and the videotape jammed in the camera. All in all, the frustrated crew spent four hours doing what should have taken them no more than one.

On another occasion, a television interview that was taking place in room 928 was interrupted by a ghostly prank. The interviewer had just asked a question about the spirit that haunted the room when a faint voice began to speak. After a moment, everyone realized that the clock radio had turned itself on.

"It must've been set to go on at a certain time," said the camera operator.

That was true—the radio had been programmed to turn on. But not for another 65 minutes. Everyone shook their heads and assumed that Montgomery Clift's ghost had just announced his presence.

Clift's spirit showed himself more forcefully during an *Entertainment Tonight* segment featuring a very skeptical interviewer. A camera light exploded and a horizontally sliding window slammed shut—both perfectly timed responses to the interviewer's cynical comments.

Others have been drawn to the Hollywood Roosevelt Hotel because of their belief in the spirit world. Many psychics and sensitive people have investigated the hotel, hoping to meet a ghost or two. Almost always, they have been successful. And often they have been able to offer explanations or greater detail about the hotel's mysterious phenomena.

Two different psychics who have examined the strange cold column in the Blossom Ballroom have sensed the spirit of a man who is dressed in black and beset by anxiety. Perhaps he was once a nervous nominee at the early Academy Awards.

Another psychic, upon walking into the Cinegrill Lounge for the first time, announced, "There's a ghost in here. It's a very strong presence. It's a man, a black man, a musician. He plays a clarinet." The Cinegrill would be an appropriate haunt for a musician, given its history as a jazz club where many of the greats got their start.

Astrology writer Linda Goodman might also be described as "psychically sensitive." She wrote her first book while staying in room 1217 and mentioned to staff that the room had "a presence, a special quality about it." It should be noted that room 1217 eventually became room 1221—the one where the phone just won't stay on the hook...

The most thorough investigation of spiritual activity at the hotel was conducted between 1992 and 1994 by well-known psychic Peter James. With a camera operator, an assistant and, on occasion, some members of the staff, James spent countless hours touring every part of the hotel. Sometimes James would work for hours with no results. More often he would manage to make contact with the entities who made the Hollywood Roosevelt their afterlife home.

According to an account on Peter James' web site (ghostencounters.com), he was able to detect approximately 35 ghosts during his two-year investigation of the hotel. He says that most of them are celebrities from Hollywood's golden era. Montgomery Clift is one of the famous phantoms that James came to know well after spending a number of nights in room 928.

During James' first stay in Clift's room, he was awakened in the middle of the night by the sensation of a heavy weight on top of him. He sensed a presence in the room and saw a shadowy figure standing beside the bed. The apparition eventually sat down in a corner chair, where it watched James for approximately 30 minutes. By the time the ghost stood up, walked across the room and vanished, Peter James was very certain that he had just been visited by Montgomery Clift. Later, James would describe Clift as "a gentle soul with a boyish nature," who remains at the Hollywood Roosevelt trying to find peace.

James' investigation showed that certain locations within the hotel were more attractive to the spirits than were others. The basement boiler room, for example, was a veritable gathering place of ghosts. While it might have lacked the sort of atmosphere required to please the living, James explained that "spirits tend to gather where there is machinery and energy." He said that the room was full of entities and was presided over by a very strong, territorial specter named either "Ron" or "Ronald."

Another area where the paranormal activity seemed concentrated was the hotel's penthouse. At the time of the investigation, it had sat unused for a number of years. But as the group entered the darkened suite, it became clear that it was far from "unoccupied."

Peter James and his camera operator, a man named Dimitri, initially entered the penthouse alone while the rest of the group waited outside the door. According to the hotel's report, as the psychic walked through the quiet rooms, he was suddenly "grabbed about the legs and held fast." While James struggled to free himself from his invisible attacker, Dimitri kept the camera rolling. The resulting dramatic footage showed Peter James wrestling with a ghost whom he came to know as "Frank." Apparently Frank had once worked as a bodyguard in the penthouse and had found it difficult to leave his responsibilities behind.

Once "Frank" allowed the group to proceed into the penthouse, other spirits were encountered there. Peter James spent some time comforting the ghost of a lost little girl, and in another room, all five people in the group listened in amazement as something that sounded like a large piece of metal was scraped across the cement floor. The noise was loud and clear, but there was nothing that could be seen causing it.

During an earlier visit, the psychic had declared that the Academy Room was also a very active area. He felt "many spirits, especially on the stairway" of the old Arthur Murray Dance Studio that adjoins the outside wall of the Academy Room. James was repeatedly drawn to that wall and asked the hotel staff, "What are they hiding here?" He felt that something of historical significance was entombed within the concrete. The group also discovered an extremely cold column in the Academy Room, which Peter James felt was "a tubular shaft where the spirits enter."

Considering the amount of paranormal activity that occurs at the hotel, that "shaft" must be the spectral equivalent of a revolving door. The unexplainable events that began following the restoration continue to fill the hotel's security log books today.

When author Barbara Smith was researching her book *Ghost Stories of Hollywood* (Lone Pine Publishing, 2000), she spent several nights at the Hollywood Roosevelt Hotel. One evening, after a tour of the city, she was sitting in bed "thinking quite reverentially about the people who had founded Hollywood." As she paused, she set down the book that she had been reading. At that moment, the lamp on the bedside table turned off. Smith felt quite comfortable in the dark—it was peaceful and quiet—so she made no move to fix the problem. Apparently there was no need to.

"After a full minute," she recalled, "the light came back on again. I felt honored to receive such a visit, and I said out loud, 'I understand—you're here.' "

It was a courteous acknowledgment and a definite understatement. The spirits of Hollywood's past obviously remain very much alive in the historic, and haunted, Hollywood Roosevelt Hotel.

CHAPTER II

Northwest Wonders

Golden North Hotel

The Golden North Hotel in Skagway, Alaska, opened its doors in 1898, promising to serve as a "first-class hotel" for the "unique clientele" of adventurers who had arrived with the gold rush. More than a century later, there are fewer cases of gold fever, but little else has changed. The Golden North is now, as it was then, "a first-class hotel." The guest rooms are charmingly appointed with authentic period furnishings, and an elegant Victorian-style restaurant serves authentic Alaskan cuisine. There is a traditional microbrewery on the premises as well, so guests can quench their thirst with a historically authentic specialty beer after a long day of touring the scenic town.

Much of the hotel's grand appeal is a result of the 1.2 million dollar renovation the proprietors, Dennis and Nancy Corrington, undertook in 1998. When they purchased the property in January 1997, the place was suffering from a notable lack of luster. Dennis Corrington recalled it as "derelict and run down and dirty and grubby…" He had also heard that it was haunted—but the proud new owner wouldn't *truly* believe that until he attempted to spend his first night there.

It was January 15, and Corrington had just closed the sale on the old hotel. When he finished work, at nearly midnight, he decided that he would celebrate the purchase by spending his first night as owner in one of the Golden North's rooms. He walked back to the empty hotel, through freshly fallen snow, and let himself in the front door.

"I set up a room on the first floor," Corrington later recalled. "I dropped off my suitcase and my shaving kit and a few things. Then I just kind of walked around in the lobby and the restaurant and the bar. It was kind of a fun feeling to have my own bar that was all set up, so I went back and cracked a beer and poured a shot of Yukon Jack. And I was standing behind the bar, sipping it, when all of a sudden I smelled this real strong perfume. And, at the same time, it got real cold in the bar."

Dennis Corrington's first thought was that the hotel's female bartender had returned from vacation, but when he called the woman's name, he received no answer. He walked to the other end of the room, searching for her, but found no one. Instead, he was overwhelmed by a strange sensation.

"I just got this real eerie, cold feeling all over my body. [I was] clammy and chilled and all the hair stood up on the back of my neck…"

At that point, Corrington remembered the ghostly story that had long been told about the Golden North Hotel.

"I thought, 'Oh, this must be Mary the ghost! That was a neat trick! Can you do that again?' And that perfume smell came back very, very strong again. It was undeniable."

Corrington felt certain that he was in the presence of something otherworldly. Not knowing what else to do, he fell back on his courteous nature. He introduced himself to the spirit, explained his presence in the hotel and mentioned that he and his wife were planning to fix the place up.

"We hope you'll like what we do, and we don't mean you any harm," he said reassuringly. Then, having spoken his piece, Dennis Corrington went back to his room.

He found it locked.

Unnerved but undaunted, Corrington rummaged around the front desk until he found the key for that

An early photo of the Golden North Hotel in Skagway, Alaska

room. He went back, opened the door and was met with the sound of rushing water.

"In the bathroom, the water was running in the sink," he explained. "It wasn't just dripping; someone had turned it on. And it was a real stiff, hard-to-turn type of faucet."

Corrington decided right then and there that he would be more comfortable spending the night in his own apartment. As he left the hotel, he noticed visible proof that his "visitor" had not been of this earth. There was only one set of footprints—his own—leading up to the door through the fresh snow.

"That was the official welcome," he later stated.

Dennis Corrington remembered hearing about "Mary the ghost" at least 20 years before he and Nancy bought the Golden North Hotel. Although he "didn't pay any attention to it," it was a well-established part of the local folklore.

According to the legend, Mary was a young woman engaged to a fellow who was seeking his fortune in the Dawson gold fields. One day she received a letter from her fiancé, which contained the wonderful news that he had "struck it rich." He asked her to meet him in Skagway, where the young couple could finally be married.

Mary packed her bags and her beautiful, white wedding dress and made the journey to Skagway. Once there, she checked into room 24 of the Golden North to await her beloved.

It turned out to be a long, sad wait. They say that Mary's man died in a dogsled accident while on his way to meet her. Mary, in a sense, died of a broken heart. She came down with pneumonia and, rather than seeking treatment, chose to put on her wedding dress and wait for death to claim her. The proprietor of the hotel eventually discovered her lying cold, still and peaceful on the bed, her white lace gown covering her like a shroud.

In *Ghosts of the Klondike* (Lynn Canal Publishing, 1993), author Shirley Jonas wrote:

> Staff and guests of the hotel have reported seeing the graceful form of a young woman in a long white gown...They have also said that they have heard footsteps in the night going down the long carpeted hallways and a rustling sound quite similar to that of an old-fashioned petticoat...Perhaps Mary's gentle spirit is still waiting for her wedding day?

Some people who have visited the Golden North Hotel have been haunted in a less "gentle" manner, however—

leading many people to speculate that there is more than one resident ghost. A woman named Sharon Garland told Shirley Jonas about a frightening encounter she had at the hotel while on a family vacation.

On the second night of Garland's stay, she became very suddenly, alarmingly ill. She was vomiting and periodically losing consciousness. Her husband was so concerned that he wanted to charter a plane to take her to Juneau and the nearest doctor. But the weather was uncooperative, and Garland decided to "hold off for a while" to see if her illness would pass.

Eventually she fell asleep. When she awoke, her eyes were drawn to a hazy, pulsating light form standing in front of the hotel room door. Garland later described it as having "substance" and "human form" but noted that she could see through the light and could not tell if it was male or female.

"What *is* that?" she asked her husband.

"I don't know..." he replied, "but I've been watching it for two hours!"

Eventually the mysterious light disappeared. Sharon Garland was amazed to discover that the instant it was gone, she felt perfectly well again.

Several days later, Garland was recounting her strange experience as she trimmed a young man's hair in her hairdressing salon in Juneau. The customer listened for a while, then told Garland, "Wait a minute. Stop cutting my hair." He then turned to his friend and said "Are you listening to this? This is spooky—this is really weird." It turned out that he had experienced an identical illness while staying in the same hotel, although his health had been otherwise perfect for years.

Garland and her family eventually moved to Skagway, where she had plenty of opportunities to hear about other ghostly goings-on at the Golden North. Sometimes the stories seemed eerily familiar. There was one occasion when she overheard a young couple saying that they had been staying at the hotel but had been so badly frightened by a strange "light form" that they had checked out in the middle of the night.

Other people have reported having "unsettling" experiences. One man awoke from a sound sleep because he felt that he was being choked. At the same time, he felt immense pressure on his chest. One has to wonder: was the fellow being attacked by some aggressive entity, or was he experiencing symptoms of the pneumonia that killed Mary in 1898? The guest was sleeping in room 24, where Mary is believed to have died.

While paranormal activity has been witnessed throughout the hotel, room 24 does stand out as being somewhat "special." Nancy Corrington remembered hearing that the previous owners had not been able to keep the window in that room closed—even when the window was securely locked and the room was vacant. Then there was the time an unkempt-looking man wandered in off the street and went directly to the third floor. The Corringtons' manager followed and found the stranger in the hallway with tarot cards spread out around him. He said that "the spirit" had drawn him in. He was sitting outside room 24. It is also worthy of note that Nancy and Dennis Corrington spent their wedding night in room 24 of the Golden North back in 1985.

"We didn't even realize that it was haunted," said Nancy. "We had no experience whatsoever at that time that would make us think there was any sort of spiritual being there—but, at the same time, it enticed us to eventually purchase the hotel."

Could Mary have known that the Corringtons would be the people to restore her home to its former glory? The spirit did appear to be very involved in the renovation. Often she was a nuisance, causing tools and other items to move or vanish just when the workmen needed to use them. But Mary did her best to be helpful too, as Dennis Corrington recalled.

"There was one fellow, Paul, who was carrying a large load of something into the hotel. As he approached the door, he thought, *How am I going to get the door open?* Just then, the door opened, and there was nobody there. So he walked in with his load, and he turned around and looked at the door, and then the door closed. So he just said, 'Thank you, Mary.' "

When Mary tried to similarly "assist" Nancy Corrington with the decorating of the hotel, it was more of a frustrating experience. After making all of her color, fabric and wallpaper selections, Nancy flew back to the Corringtons' winter home in St. Louis. When she arrived, however, she was dismayed to discover that the sample books she had so carefully packed had simply vanished out of her luggage.

"Everybody in the hotel was looking all over for the stuff," she said. "For about three days…they went through drawers and rooms and didn't find anything. Finally, on the fourth day, all the wallpaper samples, all the carpet samples, all the books were found lying open at the top of the third-floor stairway."

The wallpaper book had been opened to the selection

that Nancy Corrington had chosen—but a different sample lay over top of it. Nancy interpreted it to be Mary's choice and bowed to the ghost's decorating judgment.

"We used the paper that we figured Mary must have picked," she said. "We didn't dare go with the first one."

Though Mary has occasionally inconvenienced the Corringtons, they have never considered having any sort of ceremony to clear her spirit from the premises. Quite the contrary, they seem to respect her right to be there.

"She came with the territory," Dennis Corrington says.

Nancy Corrington agrees.

"I think she watches things kind of closely," she says. "And, besides, I kind of like her!"

It sounds as though Mary will be welcome to stay on as long as she likes in room 24 of the Golden North Hotel.

Hot Lake Hotel

It's easy to see how the ghost stories might have started. Hot Lake Hotel itself looks like a ghost. Over the decades, what remains of the resort and sanitarium that was once popularized as "the Mayo Clinic of the West" has often sat empty, enshrouded by mist that rises from the scalding mineral waters that once gave the place its life. People who have seen the hotel this way—vacant, abandoned and half-hidden within a veil of steam—say that it is difficult to imagine it in its heyday. But there was a time when shiny Packards, Duesenbergs and Buicks filled the parking lot, and the daily train would roar up to the covered platform to deliver scores of passengers who had

Hot Lake Hotel prior to the 1934 fire that leveled the wooden portion of the structure (seen at the right)

come to rest and partake of Hot Lake's reputedly healing waters. That time was early in the 20th century, when a visionary doctor named W.T. Phy turned a natural phenomenon into a booming business.

Hot Lake, situated between the towns of Union and La Grande in eastern Oregon, is so named because of the 2,500,000 gallons of boiling spring water that feed it daily. It had served as a natural spa for Native American tribes for countless generations when it was "discovered" by European explorers who came out on the Oregon Trail.

These pioneers, who encountered the simmering lake early in the 1800s, found it to be a therapeutic rest stop for their tired crews. Early on, its commercial value was appreciated. Enterprising men began carving crude tubs from fallen logs and would charge their fellow travelers 25 cents for a soothing, hot bath.

Two pioneers named Fitzgerald and Neward are said to have claimed a piece of land near the lake by 1850, and by 1864 there was a small hotel on the site. It catered to the newly wealthy lumber barons and mining moguls who came to enjoy the salubrious effects of the geothermically heated waters. In 1907 a man named Walter Pierce (who would later enjoy political success as governor of Oregon and a member of Congress) built the brick structure that stands today. The 105 rooms were heated by a network of pipes carrying the readily available, 208-degree spring water. Pierce's "Hot Lake Resort" was respectably successful, earning nearly $180,000 per year in a time when room rates were $3.50 per week and meals cost a quarter. But it wasn't until 1917, when the resort came under the directorship of Dr. W.T. Phy, that business began to boom. Phy implemented several changes and added a third-floor surgery room. Soon Hot Lake was widely known as a hospital, as well as a resort. People from across the country flocked to take advantage of the waters, which Dr. Phy claimed held curative powers for sufferers of ailments ranging from syphilis and alcoholism to arthritis and depression. An extensive wooden addition to the original brick building was built to accommodate the huge numbers of tourists and medical patients who visited Hot Lake. There were luxurious accommodations for more than 300 and kitchen facilities that served thousands of meals per day. There was a ballroom, a poolroom, a barber shop, a commissary, a confectionery, solariums and, of course, bath houses where one could indulge in soak, sweat, mud and sauna treatments. By 1924 Dr. Phy's combination of vacation resort and therapeutic treatment center greeted an average of 124 new guests each day. A mere 10 years later, Hot Lake Hotel stood in both structural and financial ruin.

The resort's decline began with the Great Depression. The institution was already sinking beneath a heavy load of debt when, in 1932, there came another devastating blow: the death of Dr. Phy. Phy's son attempted to take the helm. He had applied for a consolidation loan to rescue the business when fate dealt the deciding blow in 1934. A devastating fire leveled the entire wooden portion of the resort. The frame structure was never rebuilt, and the fire marked the end of Hot Lake Hotel's glory days.

Since then, the property with its original brick building has seen a succession of owners and served a variety of functions. For a time following the fire, it still operated as a resort hotel. In the early 1950s it was transformed into a retirement home. In 1974 that closed and a portion of the lower floor opened as a restaurant. In the early 1980s the place operated briefly as a small spa. Over the years there were valiant attempts at restoration and numerous proposals to reopen the resort or convert the property to some other purpose. But nothing ever managed to take hold. Nothing, that is, except the stories that Hot Lake Hotel was not quite as vacant as it looked…

Rumors began to circulate in the mid '70s, just after the retirement home closed for good. Once the third-floor facility was bereft of its human tenants, some other presence seemed to settle comfortably into place. There were stories of doors slamming inexplicably, terrible groaning noises and concentrated pockets of extremely chilled air. These initial stories might have been based upon nothing more than the sounds and sensations of a deserted, drafty old building. But other phenomena, more difficult to explain, began to happen as new people came to live and work in the three-story brick haunt.

Donna and Dave Pattee were part owners of Hot Lake Hotel for a few years in the 1970s. They ran a restaurant in the building and attempted to refurbish a number of the guest rooms. Though the Pattees generally stopped short of saying that they believed the ghost stories, they had to admit that there were many incidents at Hot Lake which could not be explained.

Donna Pattee found it easy to dismiss vague rumors but had to seriously consider the stories reported to her by people she trusted. One waitress who worked in the restaurant said that she had heard eerie piano music drifting down from the empty third floor of the building. Another, who lived alone in a room on the second floor, was unnerved at night by ghostly conversations that filtered through her walls from vacant rooms. Even an accountant friend of the Pattees who stayed in a first-floor apartment told the couple that he had been "disturbed" by the paranormal occurrences. For Donna Pattee, however, the most believable tales were likely the ones told to her by her own mother, who acted as a caretaker and lived on the first floor.

"She swore she heard people walking in the hallway at night," Pattee told Curt Asher in an article for the *La Grande Observer* (May 18, 1995). She hinted at her mother's credibility when she added, "My mother wasn't the type to get spooked, either."

After a while, Donna Pattee was able to add her own mysterious experiences to the growing list. She found three rocking chairs on the third floor that never collected dust. Those same chairs also tended to reposition themselves in the room when no one was looking. The Pattees were at a loss to explain how that happened. They also had to wonder who constantly shut off lights that Donna had made a point of turning on.

There were no easy answers to the Pattees' questions. But they didn't have to go far to find someone who believed their stories. A fellow named Richard Owens worked at Hot Lake Hotel as a caretaker and handyman. He and his wife lived in a second-floor suite for some time in the '70s. The things that happened to them there created vivid, disturbing memories for the couple.

One particular phenomenon occurred every evening, just after Owens and his wife went to bed. Around 10 PM, the couple would lie awake together and listen as echoing footsteps traveled down the long, dark hallway that led to their room. Once the footsteps reached the bedroom door, they would cease—until the same time the following night.

One night, Richard Owens decided to surprise the ghostly visitor. He waited behind the door after his wife retired and waited for the footsteps to begin. They did, as usual, at the far end of the hallway. As the sound grew closer, Owens grew more excited. He believed that he was about to solve the long-standing mystery. When the footsteps stopped outside the door, Owens yanked it open. To his disappointment and unease, he found nothing there except the long, deserted hallway.

It wasn't long before Owens possessed a riveting repertoire of haunting stories about Hot Lake. He often spoke of the piano that played by itself on the locked and empty third floor. The piano chair often moved around of its own volition, and sheet music that was stored beneath the seat sometimes ended up on the music stand. That, however, disturbed Richard Owens far less than the piercing screams he often heard coming from the white-tiled room that had been the third-floor surgery.

The third floor seemed to be where the anomalous activity was concentrated. Owens would sometimes see lights glowing in the upper windows although there was no electricity there. And sometimes on the hottest summer days, he would encounter a freezing cold pocket of air as he tended to some upstairs duty.

Richard Owens preferred it when his duties did *not* require him to be on the third floor—particularly at night. Unfortunately, leaks in the roof meant that when it rained, no matter what hour of the day or night it was, Owens had to make trips to the third floor to check and empty his strategically placed buckets. One stormy night, as he walked through the darkened halls wielding only a flashlight for protection, he could not shake the creepy sensation that he was being watched.

Owens was trying to dismiss his paranoia as he walked past a row of old-fashioned, high-backed wheelchairs. But then he heard a noise—a stealthy, squeaking sound. He turned around to see that one of the chairs had rolled out of formation and had begun to follow him down the hall. (That Richard and Linda Owens did not move out that very night stands as perhaps the *most* unbelievable event to ever occur at the Hot Lake Hotel.)

Another night, in the spring of 1977, Richard Owens was once again "followed" down one of the third-floor halls by a supposedly inanimate object. That time, it was a fire hose that came loose from its moorings on the wall and slithered after him like a large, gray snake. The next day, Owens realized that the hose incident had taken place on the anniversary of the devastating 1934 fire. He later told the *La Grande Observer*, "Every year on the anniversary of that fire, you could go out there and something weird would happen."

Sometimes "something weird" could be experienced just by driving past the old building. Over the years, many motorists have reported to police that a wild-eyed old man had jumped in front of their vehicle as they passed the overgrown entrance to the vacant hotel. Some swore that they drove right *through* the man, who tends to be seen on particularly windy, moonless nights. Is this the specter of some hapless patient whose depression was not eased by the soothing mineral waters? Or could it be the ghost of Dr. W.T. Phy, jealously guarding his renowned sanitarium? The apparition makes one stop and realize that few people have bothered to theorize publicly about the identities of the spirits who inhabit Hot Lake Hotel.

Dave Pattee offered his general opinion in the October 27, 1977, *La Grande Observer*. "Oh, I think a lot of people have expired before their time in this building—you bet they did. You can't have a building of this age and this history without a ghost or two," Pattee said. "It wouldn't be right."

Especially now, since the building has deteriorated into something completely unfit for the living. According to one La Grande resident, the nearly century-old brick building is now "...very torn down. The windows are all knocked out. It's quite sad." Given the natural amenities and convenient location of the property, it seems odd that none of the businesses attempted there over the last three decades have met with lasting success.

Today there is an RV park on the lake. It is the only option for those who wish to enjoy an extended stay near the steaming waters of Hot Lake or near the haunted ruin that was once considered "the Mayo Clinic of the West."

Kootenay Hotel

Some ghosts, it would seem, like to play with matches. It's a dangerous form of amusement—and legend has it that there are at least three hotels in western North America that have suffered the fiery consequences of their phantoms' actions.

Chateau Lake Louise in Alberta displays a photograph of the blaze that all but destroyed the hotel in 1924, and the photo includes a misty image that hotel staff of the day identified as their resident ghost. Those who recognized the playful spirit assumed that he had started the fire and then stayed behind to mingle with the crowd watching his destructive handiwork.

The Willow Hotel in Jamestown, California, survived a holocaust that virtually leveled the entire town in 1896, only to become haunted by angry spirits of townsfolk who had perished in the blaze. The ghosts seemed to think that the hotel should have burned as well and devoted themselves to making that happen. The hotel was plagued by countless fires throughout the 1900s. Eventually the owners gave up trying to rebuild the guest room portion of the building and simply maintained the restaurant and bar.

And roughly 30 miles from the Yukon border in the northern British Columbia community of Atlin is yet another story of a hotel that may have been brought down by a ghostly desire for fire. It is the story of the Kootenay Hotel.

Those who are familiar with Atlin's history might say that the hotel was simply in the habit of burning down. In the early years, townspeople had to gather together twice to rebuild the Kootenay—both times following fires that had swept through the entire town. But the third Kootenay Hotel proved more enduring. It was built in 1917 and served Atlin for many decades. At one point, it seemed to become the permanent home of a spectral guest.

Diane Smith first heard the story in the late fall of 1968, when she and her husband became the new owners of the Kootenay Hotel.

"At one time, the Indians from the Telegraph [Creek] area were taken to Whitehorse for medical treatment," she wrote. "Usually they were flown to Atlin in one of the bush planes and then probably driven the rest of the way on the mail bus. They had to overnight here, and they stayed at the Kootenay Hotel."

According to Smith, one regular traveler was an elderly Native woman who loved to smoke but could not be trusted with her own matches. The proprietor of the hotel at that time offered a thoughtful solution. He always booked the woman into room 11, directly above the office. When the old lady wanted a cigarette, she simply tapped on the floor with her cane. The proprietor, upon hearing the signal, would go upstairs and give her a light.

One night, the man was busy and took a little longer than usual to answer the woman's signal. When he opened the door to room 11, he realized that he was much too late. The old lady was dead, still sitting with her cane in her hand.

"After that happened," Diane Smith explained, "a tapping sound was often heard coming from room 11 or nearby. I never heard it, but one of my staff claimed she did. A telephone company man who occupied the room across the hall for a period of time told us he heard it at the same time each night."

Over the years, several people tried to find a logical explanation for the tapping. One woman crawled on hands and knees through every inch of the attic, looking for anything that might have been bumping or scraping on the ceiling. Another time, the entire exterior of the hotel was examined for wires, loose siding or anything that might have been moving rhythmically in the wind. No explanation for the tapping in room 11 was ever found.

As for Diane Smith, she saw no need to rid the Kootenay of its unusual phenomenon.

"I certainly didn't mind sharing the hotel with a ghostly guest," she claimed. "She didn't take up any space, and most people who used room 11 never heard her. [Also,] no one ever saw her."

As it happened, no one ever would. In late November 1969, just one year after Smith and her husband bought the Kootenay Hotel, it burned to the ground. On this one piece of Atlin property, there had been three Kootenay Hotels and three horrible fires. After the third blaze, no one had the heart to rebuild.

As for the old woman's ghost, Diane Smith wrote, "As far as I know, she has not been heard from again. Maybe she just went home to Telegraph Creek."

Or maybe she was satisfied that someone finally brought her a light.

Manresa Castle

A deep voice narrates the story in a foreboding tone. The tale is underscored with a dramatic, discordant soundtrack. The images are shadowy and blurred, with lightning-quick flashes of scenes designed to shock. The overall effect is undeniably compelling—but how close does it come to portraying to the truth?

In the early 1990s, the television show *Sightings* taped an episode about the ghosts of Manresa Castle, an elegant and historic hotel in Port Townsend, Washington. According to the program, the 19th-century castle is haunted by the spirits of two desperate people who committed suicide there. However, those who have researched the subject at the Jefferson County Historical Society's archives say that there is no documentation of a suicide ever having taken place at Manresa Castle. And the hotel's general manager, Roger O'Connor, says that the documents don't exist because the suicides never happened. He credits these "historical events" to the active imagination of a bartender who once worked at the hotel.

"He invented a couple of ghosts to entertain guests," O'Connor explained. "An unnamed Jesuit priest who [hanged] himself in the attic above room 302 and a lady named Kate who jumped to her death from room 306." According to O'Connor, it wasn't long before people began to believe the stories. Word spread, and there were many guests who booked into Manresa Castle with the hope of having a spectral encounter.

"It didn't hurt," O'Connor once told the *Bremerton Sun*, "that the ghosts inhabited two of the most expensive rooms in the hotel."

It must have seemed appropriate, too, having an authentic ghost story to complement the Gothic atmosphere of the castle. The massive, stone Victorian mansion sits on a high ridge, overlooking Port Townsend like a feudal lord. It was designed, complete with turrets, to resemble the imposing medieval castles of Europe. Today, after years of careful renovation, the hotel offers every modern comfort and convenience, yet it still looks as formidable and impressive as it did the year it was first built.

That year was 1892. The mansion was built as a private residence for Charles Eisenbeis, a prominent businessman and the first mayor of Port Townsend. In the 1920s Eisenbeis Castle, as it was then known, was sold to the Catholic Church. The priests who lived there renamed their home Manresa Hall, after the area in Spain where St. Ignatius was inspired to found the Order of Jesuits. In 1968 the mansion was sold again, renamed "Manresa Castle" (acknowledging each of its previous owners) and opened to the public first as a restaurant and then as a hotel. It is only in the last dozen years or so that it has come to be known as a haunted hotel.

Roger O'Connor is the first to admit that the haunting has been good for business. Writing about the *Sightings* episode in a hotel press release, he claims that "the major result of the show was a flood of bookings from people wanting to rent rooms 302 and 306."

Room 302 is the Turret Room, where legend tells of a tortured young Jesuit priest who hanged himself from the attic rafters. Room 306 is said to be haunted by Kate, a British maid who threw herself from the third-story window when she learned that her true love was lost at sea. Whether these tales are founded in fact or in the fertile ground of a bored bartender's imagination, it is interesting to note that some very strange things have happened in the two rooms over the years.

The general manager in 1990, Jill Tomsai, told one newspaper reporter that some members of the housekeeping staff refused to work on the third floor. They claimed that they often heard their names being softly called out while they worked and that they generally felt uncomfortable in that part of the castle. In the October 27, 1993, *Jefferson County Leader*, a former Manresa Castle housekeeper named Tammi Headley told stories about light switches that flipped on by themselves, a water glass that flew out of her hand and shattered and the time she saw two brilliant, unexplainable flashes of light from beneath the door of room 306.

A new chef who stayed at the hotel when he was first hired in the summer of 1997 had a similar experience. He mentioned seeing strange bursts of light beneath the door of his third-floor room. When he opened the door to investigate, he found the hallway empty.

Even the front desk staff, who work far from the reputedly haunted rooms, have experienced some chilling moments. Some have spoken of suddenly smelling an intense, flowery perfume when they were alone in the lobby. Some have wondered how it was that they heard furniture being loudly moved about in rooms that were locked and vacant. And all have puzzled over some of the stories that have come to them from hotel guests.

Some guests would complain about being kept awake by rowdy neighbors. Usually, however, a quick check of the hotel log would confirm that the adjoining rooms had been empty at the time. Others would mention that their

Manresa Castle, Port Townsend, Washington

possessions had been moved during the night, or that the bureau drawers had been pulled open while they slept, or that the lights had gone on and off by themselves. The desk clerks seldom knew how to respond to such odd grievances. Eventually there were so many comments that the hotel staff outfitted each of the haunted rooms with a log book and invited guests to record the odd things that happened to them.

One visitor from New Mexico wrote, "Around 3 AM

I felt the sheets tighten at my feet, the sensation one feels when someone sits down on the foot of the bed." Two women from Bremerton noted that "room 306 is kind of weird. The mirror on the vanity does strange things and the heater turns on by itself." One family wrote that at 1 AM, "blue waves of color spread across the ceiling in a circular motion" and declared it "an unusual experience!" Various other guests reported that "the lights kept going on and off," that they heard "shuffling footsteps" in the room and that "a strange glow came from the painting on the wall." One of the longer entries, written by a guest from Gladewater, Texas, offered the details of a particularly strange experience.

"We retired at about 11:30 PM," one part of the entry reads. "At 12 midnight, we heard singing coming from the bathroom. It was a woman's voice, singing a ghostly tune. Needless to say, we all woke up...I got up to go to the bathroom to see who was in there and then the door eerily came open. There was a swish of cold air and a glowing light. Then all the lights came on." The guest concluded that "it was either a ghost, or the castle has a strange way of entertaining its guests."

The log books were eventually taken out of rooms 302 and 306 because guests who had just checked in often requested a change of room after reading the entries. Only once, however, was anyone frightened enough to actually leave Manresa Castle. It happened in October 1989.

Two Canadian women were staying in room 306. One awoke in the wee hours of the morning and saw a luminescent form hovering at the foot of her bed. As the sleepy woman attempted to bring the strange image into focus, it appeared to reach out toward her with a long, glowing arm. The startled woman gasped loudly and the apparition vanished. The woman's companion awoke then too, and both listened to the hollow thumping of footsteps outside their door. A terrible odor invaded the room at that point; they would later describe it as the "stench of decay." In the end, the woman who saw the ghost stayed awake until dawn, and both women checked out promptly the next morning, although they had originally reserved the room for two nights.

But few people have been that unnerved by whatever resides in those third-floor rooms. Most who believe the stories feel that Manresa Castle offers a rare, entertaining opportunity to experience something paranormal. One Port Townsend family spends every Halloween in the Tower Room with a Ouija board, attempting to communicate with the spirit of the Jesuit priest. Some say that they have been successful.

And so the stories are ongoing—as is the debate about whether or not they are credible. The skeptics, upon hearing each tale, offer practical and scientific explanations. It has been said that a glass that has not been properly annealed in the factory will explode if its temperature changes suddenly. The strange and unpleasant odors have been attributed to a change of wind direction and the castle's proximity to a local pulp mill. The doubters like to point out that many of the guests who "see" things in the middle of the night are not wearing the contact lenses or eyeglasses they depend upon during the day. And much of what is experienced has been blamed on imagination, wishful thinking and general credulity. One man jokingly told the *Jefferson County Leader* that his "incredibly near-sighted" sister "saw a full apparition of

Kate, one night, after [she had taken] her contact lenses out and had been drinking wine." Indeed, even some of the entries in the "ghost logs" seem suspiciously contrived or at least the result of suggestion. Such examples keep the skeptics assured of their opinions.

Perhaps the most notable doubters on record are the past owners of Manresa Castle and the current general manager, Roger O'Connor—although O'Connor does concede that he may not be "susceptible to this type of activity." Nevertheless, O'Connor remains open-minded to the possibility that his workplace is truly haunted. He will even admit that he has no explanation for certain mysteries, such as the fact that the bulbs in the chandeliers often work themselves loose to the extent that they "take three turns to screw back in."

For the most part, though, the believers and the disbelievers remain in distinctly separate camps, all firmly convinced of what they "know." Conversely, any objective observer would have to admit that the legends behind the hauntings do appear to be concocted, while many of the reports of ghostly experiences seem genuine. But is it possible to reconcile these seemingly incongruent beliefs?

In her book *Ghost Stories of Washington* (Lone Pine Publishing, 2000), author Barbara Smith put forth an interesting theory. Citing the famous "Philip Experiment," in which eight members of the Toronto Psychic Society managed to create an entity where none had existed before, Smith suggested that the same phenomenon could have taken place at Manresa Castle.

> Is it possible that, as some maintain, Manresa Castle was not haunted prior to its present ownership, but

> that it is legitimately haunted now? Could it be haunted by two spirits brought to "life" through the power of human thought and will? This theory may possibly explain the strongly contradictory opinions about the presence of both Kate's and the priest's ghosts…

It is fascinating to consider. Still, there remains only one certainty. Whether or not there are ghosts, there are wonderful ghost *stories* to be enjoyed at Manresa Castle.

CHAPTER III

From the Mysterious Midwest to the Eerie East

Bullock Hotel

It's like taking a step back into the Wild West. In the historic mining town of Deadwood, South Dakota, there is a hotel so reminiscent of those colorful times, the management says that when you stay with them, "you're packing 100 years into every night." It's the Bullock Hotel, named after Deadwood's first sheriff and founding father Seth Bullock—a man who influenced the Black Hills town in the 19th century and, seemingly, continues to do so today.

The original Bullock Hotel was considered one of the finest hostelries between Minneapolis and San Francisco. That may still be true today, as the building has been meticulously restored to its original splendor. Several years ago, every inch of the hotel was either refurbished or recreated in an attempt to duplicate the authentic Victorian decor. Modern amenities were added to the guest rooms, but the rich turn-of-the-century atmosphere was maintained. In 1995 the Bullock celebrated its 100th anniversary looking very much the way it did the year it was first built.

The woman who oversaw the reconstruction was a former owner named Mary Schmit. During the time that the work was going on, Schmit and her aunt lived at the hotel. Frequently they heard their names called out when there was supposed to be no one else on site. Workmen reported a series of strange incidents, including hearing disembodied footsteps in the back hall and seeing the fleeting, shadowy image of a tall cowboy. Schmit's sister was alone in the building once when all the pots and pans in the kitchen began to clatter loudly. And no one who worked on the renovation was able to forget the time the huge mahogany bar toppled. It had been left in the lobby, awaiting installation, when it fell to the floor with a mighty crash. A number of the construction workers ran to the scene and were shocked by what they saw. The fall had literally shaken the building but the 12-foot plate glass mirror attached to the back of the bar did not break. It seemed that whatever force enjoyed spooking and tricking could also be helpful when it chose to be.

The identity of that mysterious entity became known in the spring of 1991, when a letter from England arrived at the Bullock Hotel. Addressed simply to "The Proprietors," it began:

> Dear Friends,
> Recently, a lady from Roseville called at your Hotel and mentioned my name in regard to searching for records of the life of Seth Bullock. You may not remember as she told me you were very busy refurbishing the Hotel. She suggested that I write to you direct as you may be able to help me in my search...I will try to explain my interest in Seth for you to judge in the hope you may be able to judge it in a different light. If not then I am so sorry to have troubled you.

The gracious letter was from a 70-year-old gentleman named Sandy Bullock. Bullock explained that he was a psychic medium who, for five months prior to writing the letter, had been receiving messages from a spirit named Seth Bullock. Because their last names were the same, Sandy Bullock thought that he might have been communicating with an ancestor. But, as time went on, the spirit persistently communicated thoughts of America and of the town of Deadwood—a place of which the medium had never heard.

The letter was filled with astoundingly accurate and little-known facts about Seth Bullock's place in the town's history, as well as a confession from the spirit that he had been back to Deadwood and "done a bit of haunting." On Seth's behalf, Sandy Bullock explained that the "bangings" (presumably construction) going on at the hotel were keeping him away at that time. The spirit gave assurances that he would return, though, and that they would know it was "Old Seth." That part really captured Mary Schmit's attention: "Old Seth" was how she and her aunt had been in the habit of referring to their hotel's namesake.

Sandy Bullock's lengthy letter concluded in the same humble tone with which it had begun:

> Friends, I hope this makes a bit of sense to you?? I have given you the facts as given to me without any prior knowledge of the town of Deadwood. I would be most grateful for any information on the life of Seth Bullock...Will pay any postage etc. that you may incur in helping me to gain further knowledge of Seth.
>
> Yours Sincerely,
> Sandy Bullock

The spirit of Seth Bullock had found a way to formally introduce itself to Mary Schmit and the people of Deadwood. Life at the Bullock Hotel would never be quite the same again.

It surprised no one that the frontiersman had chosen

his own hotel and the town of Deadwood as a place to spend the afterlife. Bullock had shaped the history of the town as a businessman, politician and sheriff. He was arguably the area's most outstanding citizen, being a conservationist before his time, a captain during the Spanish-American War and a U.S. Marshal. He was close friends with Teddy Roosevelt, who once called Bullock his "ideal typical American."

Despite his achievements, however, Seth Bullock was obscure to the point of being virtually non-existent in popular history. This exclusion—and the popularization of some of the seedier characters of his day—was one of the issues he raised through his communication with Sandy Bullock. According to Seth, "Calamity [Jane] was just a whore," and Wild Bill Hickok a lowly murderer. The former sheriff found it offensive that Deadwood's tourism industry had overlooked so many reputable pioneers while turning those two notorious characters into icons of the era.

As time passed, Seth Bullock was able to communicate many more messages through his medium. Mary Schmit, who had long been living with Seth's antics, gained invaluable insight into the ghost's motives.

"I was a hard taskmaster in the old days," Seth Bullock said, through Sandy. Mary Schmit laughingly noted that he continued to be so.

"It's like he's still on duty as a lawman or something," she said in 1998. According to Schmit, employees who were not meeting the former sheriff's standards ran a high risk of meeting *him.*

"When I first opened up," she explained, "I had a young 18-year-old kid working for me. I was pretty sure

Seth Bullock, considered by Theodore Roosevelt to be the "ideal typical American"

he was taking beer out the back door at night. I could never catch him doing it, but I was pretty positive that he was. But, one night, he came running out of the back room, and he was just really afraid, and he said that he had seen a cowboy leaning in the doorway. A big, tall cowboy. And he knew that he wasn't real because when he turned to look at him, his face was blurred. He was just shaking with fear, and he quit."

Immediately thereafter, Mary Schmit's beer inventory stabilized. The sheriff had gotten his man.

Schmit also spoke of "a little housekeeper who just loved MTV, and from room to room she'd go in and put it on, but she could never get the TVs to stay on." When the girl complained about this one day, Mary Schmit told her,

"Don't you get it? You are not supposed to be watching MTV! He wants you to work!"

Though Seth spends much of his time keeping the Bullock Hotel's employees on their toes, guests have not been exempt from stern displays of his disapproval. Mary Schmit recalled one particular woman who was demanding and unpleasant with the staff from the moment she first checked in. At about four o'clock the following morning, Seth Bullock let the woman know what he thought of her behavior.

"She woke up," said Schmit, "and there was this tall cowboy standing at the end of her bed." The woman watched in disbelief as the forbidding-looking figure slowly faded away, then she threw on her clothes and ran down to the front desk.

"She was just blithering, you know, that there was a tall cowboy in her room," Schmit laughed. "And the night clerk goes, 'Yeah, well, that would be Seth.' "

The woman checked out immediately, and everyone on staff laughed that Seth hadn't liked the miserable guest any more than they had.

In his communications with Sandy Bullock, Seth tended to concentrate on greater concerns, however. Not surprisingly, one of the former sheriff's favorite topics was law enforcement in Deadwood. Citing the lawlessness that had accompanied the town's 19th-century gold rush, Seth was certain that the casinos that were drawing tourists to Deadwood in greater and greater numbers would result in rising crime. Sandy Bullock wrote about Seth's worries:

> Lately he is very worried about the state of the law?? He says that Deadwood is being turned into another

> Las Vagas [sic]—and there will be another influx, like the gold rush days??? He wants the present sheriff to badger the powers that be for more help...

Seth was absolutely right about the "influx," as well as the necessity for additional police. The little town with its population of 1800 began seeing up to 1.5 million tourists every year. It followed that there were more incidents of crime, which, according to Mary Schmit, "is going to happen any time you start putting that many additional bodies through a town." Fortunately, Schmit added, "they rose to the occasion and hired a small army. So there really weren't any problems."

Seth must have been pleased with the swift action, although it likely wasn't in response to his advice.

"Oh, it wasn't because Seth said to do it," said Mary Schmit. "It was just because they had so much money."

Over the years, when he wasn't concerning himself with crime rates or the work ethic of hotel employees, "Old Seth" often displayed a softer, more kindly side. Sandy Bullock often assured Mary Schmit that the spirit watched over her like a guardian angel. He would take care of others as well, particularly if they were children. Schmit recalled one time when Seth helped a youngster who was lost.

"We had a little boy whose parents were downstairs, and they handed him the key to the room," she said. "He was probably no more than five years old, and they handed him the key to the room and told him to go on up. Well, he's wandering around the hotel and has no idea where his room is. But he said a man came up to him and asked him if he was lost."

The child told the stranger that he *was* lost and showed him his room key. The man looked at the number on the key, led the little boy down the hallway and pointed at a door. He told the child, "That's your room."

"The next morning," Schmit recalled, "the parents were kind of curious as to who it was who had helped their son. So they were asking the front desk if they knew of anyone who would have helped their little boy, and they were trying to describe him, based upon the child's description.

"Now we have pictures of Seth everywhere," said Mary Schmit. "And at that point, while the parents were describing Seth to the desk clerk, this little kid pointed up to this big portrait we have of him and said, 'Oh, that's the man who helped me.' "

That experience, along with others, led Schmit to believe that Seth Bullock was fond of children.

"There was another instance," she said, "where another little boy was in a bathroom. He went into the bathroom and shut the door and just started talking away. He was talking, talking, talking—and when he finally came out of the bathroom, his grandparents asked him 'Who were you talking to?' And he said, 'The cowboy.' "

Whenever "the cowboy" was intent upon getting someone's attention, however, he tended to be far less kindly and subtle in his approach.

"[That's when] bar glasses and coffee cups fly through the air," said Schmit. "If he just wants to play around with you, then little fun things happen. But if he really wants to get your attention, things fly through the air. And it works pretty well."

Similar dramatics certainly worked pretty well with one blackjack dealer at the hotel who was outspokenly

The Bullock Hotel in Deadwood, South Dakota—
founded and now haunted by the town's first sheriff

skeptical about Seth's existence. Mary Schmit recalled the incident that made him a believer.

"One night he was out there at two o'clock in the morning, dealing to a full table. And somebody was asking him 'Well, have you ever seen Seth?' He goes, 'No, no—that's just a bunch of [nonsense].' He went on, just really dismissing Seth, dismissing the whole thing—and suddenly there was this loud slam. A thousand-pound candy-cigarette machine that sits clear in the back corner just started rocking and rolling. It had come out about a foot away from the wall. And the whole table turned around and watched this thing just move, you know, swaying back and forth. And then one of them went up and looked at it and said, 'You can see a hand print on it! You can see a hand print!' " Apparently the dealer in question consumed a pot of coffee before his shift was over. If he had any remaining doubts about the presence of Seth Bullock's spirit, he kept them to himself.

On a number of occasions, Seth used his energy to try to convey important messages to Mary Schmit. Once, it was a plea for help.

"There was an incident with Sandy Bullock in England," Schmit said. "He slipped and fell and lay beside his bed for three or four days. Here, the glasses were flying and coffee pots were flying and things like that."

Schmit felt that something was amiss, so she tried repeatedly to call Sandy Bullock.

"I was calling and calling and getting no answer," she said. "Then I found out, some time later, that he had lain beside his bed for three days before somebody found him."

Mary Schmit's concern for the elderly medium was genuine. Through the course of their correspondence, the two had forged a friendship. In 1992 they finally met, when Sandy Bullock made his first-ever trip to America—and to the Bullock Hotel.

"When he came over, *Unsolved Mysteries* came in and did a little segment on the story," recalled Schmit. "And it was interesting because, you know, they offered to pay him, but he refused any money. He says if you take money, you lose the connection. And he's not a wealthy man, by any means."

Those in Deadwood who had come to know Sandy

Bullock were not surprised by his refusal to profit from the story. From the beginning, the English medium had been unremittingly humble, sincere and believable. Mary Schmit's brother, John Schmit, had been convinced of Sandy Bullock's authenticity early on. He had traveled to England in 1991, the month after his sister had received the intriguing letter, and had visited with the psychic in his small, modestly furnished flat.

"Now John is very straight, you know," Mary Schmit explained. "He's very military (John Schmit was a major in the reserves at that time, with top military clearance) and very matter-of-fact. And he was very taken by Sandy. He came back and just basically said, 'That guy's for real. There's nothing fake about him.' "

What may have convinced John Schmit more than anything else was Sandy Bullock's response to a casual question Schmit posed at the end of the three-hour visit. As he was on his way out the door, he turned and asked Sandy Bullock if there was anything that he could do for Seth. The medium bowed his head and was silent for a moment. Then, in a deep voice unlike his own, he said, "There's no gate on my grave."

The response was a cryptic one, and it stayed on John Schmit's mind until the next time he spoke to his sister on the telephone. During that conversation, he asked her to describe Seth Bullock's gravesite.

"Well, it's high up on a hill above the other graves," Mary Schmit explained. "It faces towards Roosevelt Mountain. There's a bench there and a fence around it."

Mary Schmit paused then, and her brother asked her if there was any other detail that she could remember. After a few seconds, she thought of something.

"Yes," she replied. "There's no gate on his grave."

Seth's spirit, speaking through Sandy Bullock, once said, "I know it's hard for earthly souls to realize that we live on after the death of the physical body, but we do. I can roam, in spirit, through Deadwood and the Black Hills as I did in my earthly life."

Through his "roaming," Seth Bullock has played a large role in the rebirth of the hotel that he built and the town he helped to found. And his spirit still seems to be drawn there. Though Mary Schmit has now moved on, her "guardian angel" continues to be seen at the hotel. And, according to the latest stories, Seth is not alone. The spectral image of a little girl has been also been seen in the hotel's basement. There is no way of knowing who she is, though, because, sadly, Sandy Bullock recently passed away. The current management of the hotel is hoping that they might eventually find another medium who will be able to help them communicate with both Seth and the child.

Until then, they simply hope that "Old Seth" chooses to stick around the Bullock Hotel. After all, it's much easier to pack 100 years of Wild West history into every night when you can see a tall, handsome cowboy standing in the shadows.

The Olde Angel Inn

The owners of the Olde Angel Inn in Niagara-on-the-Lake, Ontario, are not shy about the fact that their establishment is haunted. An invitation on their web site clearly demonstrates that.

"Enjoy our hospitality," it reads, "and maybe you'll have an encounter with Captain Swayze, our resident ghost."

Such openness is likely born of the belief that the ghost predates the inn itself and, therefore, has every right to be there.

The original building on the site was a three-room log structure called the Harmonious Coach House. It was founded in 1789, when Niagara-on-the-Lake was called Newark. The Coach House was burned to the ground during the War of 1812, and it is believed that a wounded British soldier named Captain Swayze was hiding in the cellar at the time. When the inn was rebuilt after the war, a strange, invisible presence soon made itself known. Eventually a psychic identified the phantom as the unfortunate Captain Swayze.

For generations now, the Captain has haunted the Olde Angel Inn. One former owner described him as "a mischievous, earthbound spirit, earthbound through suffering." Though he may have suffered grievously in his lifetime, the ghost is enjoying a most comfortable home in his afterlife. The Olde Angel Inn is warm and welcoming, decorated in the cozy colonial style of Captain Swayze's day. There are plenty of heavy, exposed, hand-hewn beams and sturdy, thick plank floors. The rooms have quaint canopy beds, and the popular English pub invites guests to relax with a frosty mug and a hearty snack. The spectral British soldier must feel quite at home in such an atmosphere; at least, everyone hopes so. For having a "resident ghost," as the owners like to phrase it, certainly adds to the inn's historical appeal.

It makes for entertaining story-swapping in the pub, too. Locals and staff alike enjoy telling tales about their various ghostly encounters. Legend has it that over the decades, a number of people have seen Captain Swayze—a filmy apparition of a man in 19th-century military dress and a wig. Once, following a historical re-enactment of a local battle in the War of 1812, a server reported to her co-workers that one of the costumed actors was "still walking about down there" in the cellar. The server's complaint was checked out immediately, and the cellar was found to be absolutely deserted.

More often, however, Captain Swayze prefers to make himself known through his actions rather than his appearance. The ghost loves to rattle dishes and fling open the heavy cupboard doors. He has been known to make saucers float across the room and once hurled a beer stein at a staff member who was in the midst of a heated argument. It was through similar poltergeist antics that the spectral captain introduced himself to the current owner, Peter Ling.

Peter Ling purchased the Olde Angel Inn in the early 1990s. Having heard all of the stories about Captain Swayze, he jokingly mentioned to some patrons, "I'd like to meet this ghost." In a letter written several years later, Ling described the fascinating experience that followed:

> I was staying overnight in the oldest part of the inn, all alone. It was a cold and stormy night, with no

> moon. I was awakened around 3 AM by a terrible crash! Upon investigation, I eventually discovered that a large iron horseshoe which I had brought to the inn for luck, and which had been nailed above the fireplace, had been wrenched from the wall and hurled across the room, where it ended up facing the inn door. All the doors and windows were locked. In the morning, when I retrieved the horseshoe, there on the inn's step was a copy of the local *Niagara Advance* newspaper. The headline read "New Owner of The Angel Inn Wants to Meet Captain Swayze."

Ling drily concluded his story by writing, "I considered myself to be introduced."

According to one employee at the Olde Angel Inn, "Captain Swayze has actually been pretty quiet" in recent months. "I think he's enjoying the peace of a quiet winter in Niagara-on-the-Lake," she explained. Likely everyone is hoping that this is the case: that the ghost is merely resting and not absent. It goes without saying that it would be a shame to lose the most famous and popular patron of this charming, historic inn.

Queen Elizabeth Hotel

When Montreal's Queen Elizabeth Hotel opened its doors in April 1958, it became instantly famous as the largest new hotel in the world. Eleven years later, it made headlines once more as newlyweds John Lennon and Yoko Ono occupied a 17th-floor suite during their week-long bed-in for peace. Eventually the Queen Elizabeth would acquire another odd claim to fame—it would become known as the scene of one of the best-known and most credible ghost stories in Canadian folklore.

In 1961 a notable Montreal journalist named Pierrette Champoux was attending a conference at the luxurious hotel. On the Saturday of the event, following a luncheon, Champoux was pleasantly surprised when she met a fellow journalist named Emile Hamel. Not only was Hamel at journalist, he had been a friend of Champoux's for some 20 years. Champoux vaguely wondered why he hadn't told her that he was planning to attend the conference. She didn't bother to ask, though. Instead, the friends spent nearly 30 minutes in pleasant conversation about nothing of particular importance. When Champoux realized that she was running late for her next meeting, the two friends said their goodbyes. Hamel reached out to give Champoux's arm an affectionate squeeze before he went on his way.

During the remainder of the conference, each time Champoux thought about the chance meeting with her friend, she felt quite cheered. Still, she wondered why Hamel had not told her that he would be at the hotel. She reasoned that there had to be some logical explanation. Indeed, she had sensed that Hamel had been about to change the topic to something more serious when they had run out of time.

I'm sure he was about to explain to me why he hadn't called, Champoux told herself and she put the matter out of her head.

Two days later, Pierrette Champoux learned the truth when she received some sad and startling news. Her friend, Emile Hamel, had died. That in itself was tremendously shocking. But Champoux also discovered that Hamel's time of death had been early the previous Saturday morning—about six hours before she had enjoyed a lengthy chat with him at the hotel.

In the years since, many people have speculated that Pierrette Champoux had been absolutely correct when she sensed that her friend had wanted to speak to her about something important. In all likelihood, he must have wanted to tell her that he would not be seeing her again. It was clear that Emile Hamel's spirit had sought his friend out for one last goodbye. Around the world, there have been many such stories of loved ones appearing after death to bid a final farewell, but few, if any, match this tale in terms of astonishing detail.

There has been nothing to suggest that the ghost of Emile Hamel remains at the hotel, or that the Queen Elizabeth Hotel is in any way haunted. Quite clearly, Hamel's spirit was there because of Pierrette Champoux and not because of the location. Still, the Queen Elizabeth Hotel remains worthy of mention as the scene of this extraordinary supernatural experience.

The Lizzie Borden Bed and Breakfast

Lizzie Borden took an axe
And gave her mother 40 whacks
And when she saw what she had done
She gave her father 41

The truth is, a person simply cannot rely upon popular playground verses to deliver the cold, hard facts. According to the pathologist's report, Abby Borden received no more than 19 blows to her skull, and Andrew Borden was done in by a mere 11. According to the jury on the case, Lizzie wasn't even the one to wield the axe. The jury acquitted her after deliberating for less than an hour. So while the popular ditty is memorable, it is constructed of misinformation and may even be libelous. It's best to look elsewhere for the real details—and the Bordens' home town of Fall River, Massachusetts, is the best place to start.

A mini-industry has sprung up around the Borden case, and Fall River is at the center of it. The double murder, which took place more than a century ago, remains one of the most intriguing unsolved cases in American history. Borden artifacts, books, movies and memorabilia of all kinds are extremely popular—particularly in the town where the homicides took place. Those who dare to can now spend a night at the scene of the crime. The original Borden house at 92 Second Street is now "The Lizzie Borden Bed and Breakfast," restored to look very much the way it did on that sweltering morning of August 4, 1892.

It was nearly lunchtime on that day when Lizzie screamed out for the housekeeper to come to her aid.

"Father's dead!" she shouted. "Somebody's come in and killed him!"

Andrew Borden was indeed dead. His mutilated corpse lay on the sitting room sofa where he had made himself comfortable for a midday nap no more than a half hour earlier. Upstairs, in a guest bedroom, his wife Abby had been deceased for more than two hours. Each of the victims had been bludgeoned to death.

It was a strange case from the very beginning. Despite the brutality of the crime, there was very little blood at the scene. Although the house was occupied throughout the morning, and the street in front of it was busy, no one heard or saw a thing. And, despite nothing having been stolen, Lizzie Borden insisted that there had been an intruder.

Perhaps that unlikely claim is what threw suspicion upon Lizzie herself. It was eventually noticed that she had both the opportunity to commit the murders and a suspected motive for doing so. It was believed that Andrew Borden had been thinking of willing his considerable estate to his wife instead of his daughters. It was well known that Lizzie held no affection for her stepmother—she addressed her as "Mrs. Borden"—and being passed over by her father would have infuriated her. This, along with the testimony of a pharmacist who said that Lizzie had tried to purchase a deadly poison from him only the week before, was enough to bring about an indictment.

Convicting Lizzie Borden of the murders proved to be a greater challenge. In the Victorian era, women—particularly church-going society women such as Lizzie—were considered to be dainty, fragile and generally incapable of such violence. The defense attorney played that card effectively, once referring to the solid, 32-year-old spinster as a "little girl." When all was said and done, the all-male jury found it impossible to believe the prosecution's case. Lizzie Borden was declared "not guilty" in a court of law—but would be forever damned in the court of public opinion. She was generally shunned by the people of Fall River until her death there in 1927.

The house remained a private residence until recent years when it was converted into a combination bed and breakfast and museum. The proprietors embraced the notorious history of the home and carefully restored the rooms to their appearance at the time of the murders. They filled the house with Borden memorabilia and the gift shop with Borden souvenirs. They greeted their guests each morning with a breakfast of bananas, johnny cakes, sugar cookies and coffee—which was known to be Andrew and Abby Borden's last meal. They faithfully recreated the Borden home of August 1892 and in doing so—judging by some reports—they may have awakened the spirits of the Bordens.

According to the *Unsolved Mysteries* web site (www.unsolved.com), the Lizzie Borden Bed and Breakfast has been the scene of several strange and unexplained incidents. People have reported hearing muffled conversations, the sound of a woman crying and footsteps—when no one is around. Objects seem to move about by themselves, the lights have been known to turn on and off when no one has flipped a switch and the antique wooden doors sometimes swing eerily open, as if guided by a ghostly hand.

Some people have seen sudden, human-sized impressions appear on the bed covers, as though an invisible form had lain down there. After a few moments, the covers would smooth out once more, as though that same spectral person had risen from the bed. Visitors have noticed cold spots in several of the rooms as well. Although drafts are not uncommon in such old structures, these chilled areas are suspiciously concentrated and difficult to explain.

Not surprisingly, the spirits are believed to be those of Abby and Andrew Borden. Violent or unexpected death often seems to result in a haunting, and that may be what has happened at 92 Second Street. Guests who have "met" the ghost of Abby Borden report that she is carrying on about her domestic duties, as though nothing had interrupted them. Some witnesses have seen an older woman in Victorian-era clothing dusting the furniture and making the beds in the guest room where Abby was killed. Others have been awakened by this same apparition as she smoothes their bed covers securely around them. She might be tucking them in, or she might simply be making the bed once more, oblivious to the fact that someone is occupying it.

Andrew Borden's image appeared in a photograph of the sitting room where he was murdered. When the picture was developed, it appeared nearly all black, except for the ghostly, pale image of an old man matching Borden's description.

One of the owners of the house prefers to call it "active" rather than "haunted." But, semantics aside, most agree that the past remains quite present at the fascinating Lizzie Borden Bed and Breakfast.

Echo Valley Conference Centre

The thin, faltering beam of a flashlight finds its way through the dim twists and turns of a claustrophobic basement tunnel. A huddled group of people shuffle quietly along behind it. Their eyes follow the weak, bobbing light as it bounces off stained concrete floors and ancient radiators that line the walls. The tallest members of the group duck to avoid the web of aged pipes that crisscross the low tile ceiling.

"This way to the morgue," the young man who leads the group says in an ominous tone that leaves several of his followers wide-eyed with fear and clinging to one another for reassurance.

The leader pulls at the heavy handle of a broad, dimpled metal door that looks suspiciously like a cooler. Slowly the door swings open. No one seems eager to look into the room.

"Now," says the tour guide, "I'll tell you about the time someone tried to spend an entire night in here on a dare..."

The dramatic story, told with well-practiced timing, is enough to elicit gasps of delicious fright from the audience...

• • •

A short distance north of the town of Fort Qu'Appelle, Saskatchewan, by the shores of Echo Lake, is one of that province's most unique and historic sites. Today, this complex of brick and stone buildings, with their Tudor-style timber-and-plaster accents, is known as Echo Valley Conference Centre. It is a scenic, comfortable and

Echo Valley Conference Centre, nestled in a scenic location by the shores of Echo Lake

affordable location for group events ranging from artistic retreats to corporate workshops. In years past, however, it was known as "Fort San"—short for sanatorium—and if you were a guest there, it meant that you were very ill.

They once called tuberculosis "the white plague" and "the captain of all the men of death." In this age of antibiotics and AIDS, it is difficult to imagine how a diagnosis of this bacterial infection used to terrify. Until the 1944 discovery of the drug streptomycin, however, thousands of tubercular patients every year suffered horrible deaths.

Before drug therapy, the weapons medical science had to wield against the disease were few and unimpressive by today's standards. There was bed rest, wholesome food and plenty of fresh air, no matter how low the thermometer mercury dipped. There were a few crude surgical techniques. And there was isolation—not for the good of the patient, but to prevent spread of the disease. To meet all these needs, sanatoriums, or "sans" as they were often

Pasqua Lodge, the most haunted building in the complex

called, sprang up around North America. In Saskatchewan, Fort San was the first.

Although plans for Fort San began in 1911, construction wasn't completed until the end of the First World War. Many tubercular veterans came home in need of treatment, and this patriotic issue lent appeal to the funding drive. The facility finally opened in 1919, with returning soldiers occupying over half of the available beds.

But, if World War I helped to build Fort San, World War II helped to render it obsolete. Out of that conflict came the advent of antibiotics, an effective treatment for tuberculosis. As the quality of the drugs improved, the need for sanatoriums diminished and eventually all treatment could be handled in hospitals.

In 1972 Fort San closed its doors and the grounds were sold to the provincial government for the princely sum of one dollar. The joke—according to Gus Vandepolder, the general manager of Echo Valley Conference Centre—is that the province got taken. Fort San, essentially an autonomous village of some 50 buildings, was expensive to maintain and for years was of little use.

In the '80s, the property served as a summer school of the arts and the site of an occasional convention. It still operated at a huge deficit, however, and the buildings began to fall into disrepair. Fort San was in danger of closing permanently when in 1992 the Saskatchewan Property Management Corporation began negotiating with the Canadian Department of National Defence. The latter agreed to move the Western Canadian Sea Cadet Training Program to Echo Valley, providing a much-needed major tenant and a new lease on life. Guaranteed income from the cadets each summer finally prompted the government to refurbish the site.

Eventually the place took on the appearance of a well-tended time capsule. Repairs and upgrades were made where necessary, but features such as the red-and-green checkered hospital tile in the hallways remained. So did the old-fashioned windows and the aseptic white walls. Anyone with a bit of imagination was able to stand in one of the spartan rooms and believe that the year was 1940 and that just that morning, patients on hospital cots had been wheeled through the broad doorways to the sun balconies for their fresh-air cure.

If there is a sense of timelessness within the walls of the Conference Centre, it may be because more remains of the past than old-fashioned fixtures and furniture. Over the years, the complex has gained a reputation as a haunted place. There were rumors of entire floors appearing to be lit up and bustling with activity when, in fact, they were locked and empty. People gossiped about patients and orderlies from a previous era roaming the halls late at night. There were tales of unexplained noises and disembodied voices. And such stories might have been expected to take hold. After all, isolated and antique, with its inherent history of tragedy, Fort San was Saskatchewan's version of a haunted castle.

Some of the earliest ghost stories about Echo Valley Conference Centre spread among the students who attended music camps there. Bill, a young man who spent a part of one summer there in the late '70s or early '80s, recalled a particularly unnerving experience.

It was an especially warm day, and the band had gathered on one of the lawns for their afternoon practice. When Bill realized that he had forgotten something in his room, he left his friends and ran back into the deserted lodge. But as he rifled through his luggage, he was distracted by the sound of someone singing.

It was a woman's voice, high and clear—and unexpected in a lodge that had been assigned to the men of the group. The voice was accompanied by the sound of running water, which seemed to be coming from the bathroom across the hall from Bill's room. The young musician walked over to the doorway, where he could see clearly across the hall to the line of porcelain sinks.

The woman who stood there was young and pretty and wore a rather conservative dark dress that fell past her knees. The water taps were gushing, and as she sang and washed, the woman dreamily considered her reflection in the mirror. Bill called out to her politely.

"Excuse me, ma'am. I think you're in the wrong lodge. This is the men's."

The woman gave no indication that she had heard Bill. Thinking that perhaps the sound of the running water had masked his voice, he spoke more loudly.

"Excuse me? Ma'am?"

The woman moved the second time Bill spoke. Instead of turning toward him, however, she backed away, out of his field of vision. It was then that Bill decided to approach the woman. He walked the half-dozen steps across the hall to the bathroom.

In the time that it took Bill to do that, the woman vanished.

Bill was perplexed at first, but not frightened. He stood in the bathroom trying to reason how the woman could have left his sight so quickly, how she could possibly *not* be in the bathroom or the hallway. As he tried in vain to puzzle it out, what he noticed next *did* frighten him. Bill saw that every sink in the bathroom was bone-dry.

Bill rejoined his bandmates in a great hurry then and refused to go back into the lodge until later that evening when it was comfortably filled with people.

From approximately the same time there is a story about a group of writers who had taken a Ouija board to their Echo Valley retreat. They were aware of the Conference Centre's supernatural reputation and hoped to conjure some spiritual entertainment.

What actually happened that night is difficult to determine. To this day, the participants are evidently too upset to discuss the matter openly. One man who had interviewed several of the people involved was only willing to say that the writers had summoned much more activity than they had bargained for and had frightened themselves badly.

General Manager Gus Vandepolder finds the various stories interesting but not surprising. He feels that the site's historical record makes it irresistible to those who are superstitious. And for anyone who is apt to spin a darkly tantalizing tale, there are plenty of grim statistics with which to work.

"On average, since 1919, 40 people died here...every year the place was open," Vandepolder explained. "So that's a fair number of people to have expired on site." One of the results of the mortality rate has been a "fair number" of intriguing stories about the spirits that remain on site.

There may be no one better versed in this particular collection of folklore than Bernice Desjarlais, a member of the Conference Centre's housekeeping staff. Desjarlais is able to tell her tales with unique perspective, as both an employee of the Conference Centre and a former patient of Fort San.

"I was in here when I was six years old for two years," she explained, then added that her father had been a World War II serviceman who made it home before she was able to. "I came back when I was 12," she continued. "That time, for 10 months."

As a result of her stays, Desjarlais knows every inch of the complex in a way that her co-workers do not. And, beyond knowing the landscape, she knows the legends.

Desjarlais tells stories of a spectral wheelchair, often seen in the form of a clearly defined shadow on a door in one of the lodges. She speaks of Nurse Jane, an apparition who is said to be the spirit of a distraught nurse who committed suicide while working at Fort San. And she relates the stories of guests who have awakened in the wee hours of the morning to a racket "as though someone was dragging heavy chairs and slamming heavy doors and walking up and down the hallways."

If the stories told to her didn't convince Desjarlais that her workplace was haunted, her personal experiences there did. She recalled one incident that took place in a building that has since been torn down. She and some co-workers were on their way out of the lodge when they noticed that a light had been left on at the end of the hallway. Desjarlais walked back and turned it off. "By that time, the girls were gone out the door," she explained. "I was coming back...halfway down the hallway, and I heard 'click.' I looked back, and the light was on again. I didn't stay in there too long."

For the most part, Bernice Desjarlais has always taken the ghostly incidents in stride. By the time she had been working at Echo Valley Conference Centre for a few years, however, she was hesitant to enter Pasqua Lodge by herself. And she wasn't alone in her hesitation. According to many sources, a number of staff over the years have refused to work alone or at night in that lodge, which once housed the morgue and the autopsy room; it is said to have the highest incidence of paranormal activity. Pasqua Lodge, according to Stephen LaRose of the *Regina Leader-Post,* is "the most haunted place in the haunted community."

For his article, published on December 13, 1999, LaRose interviewed a Conference Centre employee named Jay Lowe. Lowe told one story about an 18-year-old man who had taken a dare to spend a night in the basement autopsy room of Pasqua Lodge. Even with his reputation and a bet of $150 on the line, the teenager lasted only four hours. Lowe recalled that he had been "screaming to get out," but added that it might have been due to a combination of harassment and suggestion.

"There were people banging on the floor above him, and after four hours your imagination is going, too. And it was winter—the steam was going and the pipes were banging and it was hot in there, and the building shifts."

But while Lowe felt certain that there were logical explanations for the "haunting" in that particular case, he told LaRose that there were also "all kinds of situations [that he couldn't] explain."

Some guests at the Conference Centre have gone to the washroom in the middle of the night and returned to find that their bed had been made. Others complained that the overly zealous housekeeping staff had noisily begun cleaning at 4 AM—when in fact they don't start their workday until eight. Workers clad in blue or green coveralls—perhaps a uniform of the sanatorium days—are frequently sighted, although no such uniform exists among the staff today. And then there was the co-worker of Lowe's who quit after he was alone in a changing room and, one by one, the locker doors began to open by themselves.

"[He] freaked out and he won't come back to help us any more," Lowe told the *Leader-Post*.

As the eerie stories began to accumulate and interest in them grew, Gus Vandepolder and his staff decided to capitalize on them—by offering midnight ghost tours of the complex.

"It was a little bit of a risk when we first began to do it," Vandepolder said, "but it's proven to be a positive addition to our programs." Any fears that publicly acknowledging the ghosts would drive away guests were put to rest when people began to enthusiastically request the tours.

Of course some people's enthusiastic involvement went beyond the norm. In the *Regina Leader-Post* interview, Jay Lowe recalled a tour in which one woman in the group claimed to have extra-sensory perception.

"She wanted us to jack-hammer one of the basement walls," Lowe said. "She claimed that there was a body buried behind the wall." The staff no doubt thanked the woman for her insight but elected to leave the wall in question intact.

Though it is highly unlikely that any bodies are entombed in the concrete, there have long been rumors about unmarked graves in the hills. Bernice Desjarlais believes it to be true.

"Lots of times people died here and they had no family," she said. "If nobody claimed the body, they'd get buried back there in the hills, with no marker."

Officially there is no burial ground on site, yet this is one of the more persistent Fort San stories. Gus Vandepolder heard of one staff member finding a skull on the property in 1992, and many people treat the unsubstantiated rumor as a simple matter of fact.

The idea is a central theme in Veronica Eddy Brock's 1987 novel, *The Valley of Flowers.* Though the book is a work of fiction, it is nonetheless rooted in truth, based upon the author's own experience as a patient at Fort San. Several times in the novel Brock writes that for every flower planted out by the gates, the heroine had heard that "a dead body was buried back in the hills." Although this has yet to be proven as anything more than a rumor, it is an impressively widespread and enduring one.

But it is little wonder that the dark stories persist. Fort San was a medical purgatory where hundreds died and thousands suffered. Isolation, loneliness and pain were a way of life for its citizens, some of whom lost years of their lives, if not life itself.

Today, Echo Valley Conference Centre is a cheerful, sunny, inviting alter-ego to the San. By all accounts, it is a beautiful, accommodating, pleasant place to be. Why, then, are there the continued ghostly visits?

They used to say it about tubercular spots on X-rays: these shadows take time to chase away.

The Pfister Hotel

A handsomely dressed man and woman leave their hotel room on their way to a black-tie dinner. He moves toward the elevator, but she stops him by laying her hand on his arm.

"The stairs," she says. "Let's walk down that lovely flight of steps."

They descend the sweeping grand staircase, and the woman dreamily imagines past eras and the countless beautiful couples who have taken that walk before them. As she enjoys her historical reverie, she steps slightly to one side to pass a portly gentleman in an immaculate dove-gray suit. She glances at the man briefly. There is something so pleasantly familiar about his face that she turns to look again. But in the instant that has passed, he has vanished.

"Where did that man go?" the bewildered woman asks her husband.

"What man?" is his response.

It is then that she remembers where she has seen that genial, round face. There is a portrait, elsewhere in the hotel…

• • •

In 1845 a man named Guido Pfister left Germany for the bustling frontier city of Milwaukee, Wisconsin. He worked hard and was rewarded with success. Pfister established his fortune, became a leader in the community and by the late 1800s dreamed of giving something back to the place that had served him so well. The gift he envisioned was a grand hotel, "a palace for the people" as he called it. Pfister's hotel would be something the people of Milwaukee could take pride in and something they could enjoy. Sadly Guido Pfister died in 1889 before he could make his dream a reality.

Pfister's son Charles, however, was determined to see his father's vision come to life. Charles was a persistent and savvy businessman, and within a year of his father's death, construction of the Pfister Hotel had begun. Three years after that, in the spring of 1893, the Pfister welcomed its first guests.

It was immediately obvious that Charles Pfister had spared no expense and compromised no detail. The hotel, originally budgeted at $500,000, ultimately cost three times that amount. It was a record-breaking price tag—but the money had been well-spent.

The Pfister boasted every modern convenience and safety feature of the era. It was among the first hotels in the United States to run entirely on electricity and among the first to feature individual thermostatic controls in each guest room. Along with such comfort, guests slept peacefully knowing they were staying in the

The grand Pfister Hotel in Milwaukee, Wisconsin

country's very first fireproofed hotel. The Pfister was incredibly luxurious as well, noted from the very beginning for its outstanding level of service. The staff were trained to pay strict attention to every detail, and nothing was permitted to take higher priority than the comfort of a guest. And, of course, the Pfister "palace" was beautiful. The exterior was elaborately ornate, with massive granite columns and other Romanesque details. The interior was sumptuous and elegant, featuring the finest materials and the most expert craftsmanship. The corridors and common areas were gorgeously accented with original oil and watercolor paintings—a collection of Victorian artwork that would eventually become known

The lobby of the Pfister Hotel, accented with many pieces of the largest collection of 19th-century Victorian art on display in any hotel in the world

as the largest of any hotel in the world.

The Pfister Hotel was magnificent—but it was not exclusive. While it was fine enough to host royals, dignitaries and presidents (nearly every one since William McKinley has stayed there), it remained a place enjoyed not only by its guests but by its neighbors. The hotel was intended to act as a "living room" of sorts for the people of Milwaukee. Under Charles Pfister's careful leadership, it was a spectacular living room indeed.

But of course the hotel was built to outlast its namesakes. Charles Pfister eventually died and, in the decades that followed, the hotel underwent numerous changes in ownership and two extensive renovations. Yet somehow through those changing times, the Pfister's unique and uncompromising vision of hospitality was preserved as surely as if Charles Pfister had remained at the helm.

In fact, there are those who believe that he did.

For many years, there have been stories about guests

and staff who have seen, for a fleeting moment, the smiling image of Charles Pfister. He is always described as a heavy-set, tastefully dressed gentleman, and many who have seen his apparition have identified him by a portrait that hangs in the hotel. Sometimes Pfister is on the grand staircase, surveying the lobby below. At other times he is in the minstrel's gallery, overlooking the ballroom. Always, he looks pleased with what he sees: his hotel in perfect running order.

In 1998 the Pfister's chief concierge, Peter Mortensen, admitted that initially the stories he heard had an improbable, folkloric quality about them.

"When I first came here, most of the stories I had heard were somebody who had heard from somebody who had heard from somebody. It was one of those things when anytime that somebody heard a noise, or a plate would drop…people would just say, 'Oh, it's Charlie Pfister.' "

Eventually, however, Mortensen heard a firsthand, credible account from a woman who worked in the hotel's catering division.

The woman told of getting on an elevator that held one other passenger—a pleasant-looking older gentleman wearing a suit. The doors closed and the elevator began its ascent. During the ride, the woman was watching the floor numbers light up but remained aware of the man in her peripheral vision. When the elevator stopped before the woman's floor, however, she turned to allow her fellow passenger to step out. What she discovered shocked her.

"When she turned around to let him off," explained Mortensen, "there was no one there."

Not long after hearing that story, Peter Mortensen heard

another—this time, from a member of the housekeeping staff. The woman mentioned to him that she had been working alone in one of the hallways when she was approached by a gentleman matching Charles Pfister's description. According to Mortensen, it was "...one of those situations where she turned, and when she turned back again there was no one there."

Mortensen considered both accounts to be credible yet remained conservatively open-minded in his opinion of the ghost.

"Now, certainly, if those things are possible," he said, "I can't think of a more likely candidate to make a return visit. Charles Pfister was dedicated to this hotel and to the idea of it. Obviously, he committed not only a lot of money but a lot of himself as well."

Most would agree that the investment has paid off handsomely. The Pfister Hotel, now well into its second century, routinely wins coveted industry awards and is a member of the distinguished "Historic Hotels of America." It is undoubtedly successful, but is it haunted? That may never be known, and it will never matter. Peter Mortensen said it best: "Even if the ghost of Charles Pfister isn't here, the spirit of the Pfisters is certainly present at all times."

And it is that continued presence that makes the Pfister Hotel in Milwaukee a true "palace for the people."

The Phantom Inn

In June 1974 a man named Bo Linus Orsjo was hiking around Mount Lowe in California when he noticed a large building in the distance. It appeared to be a hotel but seemed quiet and unoccupied save one, lone employee sweeping the broad front steps. Orsjo assumed that the place was closed for the season and continued on his way. Later, he discovered that there had once been a resort on that site—one that had burned to the ground nearly 40 years before he "saw" it.

The incident, reported in the December 1987 issue of *FATE* magazine, is one of many existing accounts of phantom buildings. It is endlessly fascinating to speculate about how these structures of the past manage to appear in the present. Are their images the result of a wrinkle in the fabric of time? Do some places take on so much energy from those who have inhabited them that they are able to project hazy images of themselves long after their timbers and bricks have been destroyed? It's difficult to say. But there is at least one account of a spectral building that was much more than a fleeting, filmy apparition. In the October 31, 1996, *Edmonton Journal*, a man named Fred Syska told reporter Jeff Holubitsky about a time in the late 1970s when he and his future wife actually checked into a phantom motel.

"It was just like the rising sun, it was unbelievable," Syska recalled of the glowing vacancy sign that splashed its light across the highway just south of Red Deer, Alberta. The sign must have seemed like a beacon of hope to Syska and his future wife, Andrea. The two travelers had driven all the way from Vancouver; it was past midnight, and they had been unable to find a room for the night. They were exhausted and welcomed the chance to rest.

Had the couple been less desperate, they might have changed their minds upon closer inspection of the motel. It was rundown and far from spotless. The parking lot was silent and empty, as was the dimly lit office. Still, the prospect of driving any farther was more daunting than the prospect of one night in a ratty motel room. Fred Syska followed the written instructions inviting guests to deposit eight dollars in the envelope on the desk and helped himself to a key.

The couple had their choice of any unit. They settled into unit 12 and began to prepare for bed. As tired as the two were, though, it was difficult for them to relax. Fred Syska attributed the feeling to their less-than-perfect surroundings. The bedspreads weren't clean, the room was grimy and stale and there was a crumpled candy wrapper next to the Bible in the drawer of the bedside table. When Syska peered through the tiny bathroom window, he saw another row of vacant units, all eerily empty, with their doors standing slightly ajar. Still, he was more tired than he was unsettled by his surroundings. When Andrea expressed reservations about staying, he convinced her that they would be fine for one night.

Fred Syska firmly believed that—until he tried to undress. Then the horrible sensation of eyes upon him was so strong, he found that he could not force himself to remove his clothing.

"I had an incredible sense that I was being watched," he later said, as quoted in the *Journal*. "[It] went into every bone and nerve of my frame. I don't know what it was, but I thought to myself, *If I fall asleep in here, I don't know what's going to happen.*"

Andrea didn't need to be talked into leaving. The couple threw their suitcases back into the car and left.

Although the feeling that they were being watched was growing stronger with each passing minute, Fred Syska decided that he would visit the office to collect his eight dollars. He stopped the car in front of the dingy little building and dashed in to grab his money. Immediately he wished that he hadn't bothered.

"It was almost as if there was something so ominous, I didn't know what," he struggled to explain the sensation to the *Journal* reporter years later. Whatever it was that Syska sensed, he ran away from it. He ran back to Andrea in the waiting car, jumped into the driver's seat and sped away. The two drove north in silence until they reached the city of Red Deer and found another vacancy at a comfortingly ordinary motel.

Days later, Fred Syska was describing the strange experience to a friend who frequently traveled that particular stretch of highway. The friend looked puzzled and told Syska, "There's no motel there."

It turned out that his friend was absolutely correct. There was no motel where Fred Syska and Andrea had stopped. But a little bit of further investigation revealed that there had been one—years earlier. According to an RCMP officer questioned by Syska's friend, the abandoned buildings had fallen into disrepair and eventually were torn down.

The demolition took place almost a decade before Fred and Andrea nearly spent a night in the ominous, phantom motel.

Foran's Hotel

Don't make any plans to check into Foran's Hotel during your next trip to St. John's, Newfoundland. If the place ever did exist (this story leans well toward the category of legend), it was over a century ago. According to *The Encyclopedia of Ghosts and Spirits, Volume II* by John and Anne Spencer (Headline Book Publishing, 2001), Foran's Hotel may have originally occupied the site of St. John's General Post Office. Researcher and folklorist Dale Gilbert Jarvis uncovered a haunting tale said to have taken place there in 1883.

Late one night, guests of the hotel were awakened by a loud, insistent knocking sound. The source of the noise seemed to be a vacant room on the top floor, but there was nothing within that room that could account for the commotion. Hotel staff eventually gave up trying to solve the mystery and guests did their best to block out the racket and go to sleep. The incident would likely have been forgotten had it not repeated itself the following night at exactly the same hour.

Again, the guests complained. Again, staff searched for the cause of the violent knocking and a solution to the problem. Although the banging noise could be traced to the same vacant room, no one could find the cause of it.

When the clamor resumed on the third night, the hotel management knew that they had a serious problem. Perhaps because they wanted to reassure their outraged guests that some action was being taken, the management placed a double guard outside the noisy, vacant room. Coincidentally, the knocking noise ended that very night. Everyone was quite relieved, and it was agreed that the mysterious, noisy room should not ever be rented out.

Several uneventful months passed. Then one evening, a man walked into the lobby of Foran's Hotel, seeking a room for the night. Unfortunately the only vacant room in the building was the one that had been locked up following the bizarre episode of supernatural knocking. The clerk at the desk decided that, as he had no other room to offer the man, he would rent him the mysterious room rather than send him to a competing establishment. The man paid for his lodging and retired for the night.

A few hours later, the knocking began. It was even louder this time and didn't stop. Once again, every guest of the hotel was awakened, and all followed the sound to the room on the top floor. Everyone gathered around, hands clapped over their ears to block out the relentless, thundering sound. Finally a staff member used trembling hands and a master key to open the door to the room. Inside, a horrible discovery awaited the crowd. The man who had rented the mysterious room only hours earlier was lying still, cold and dead on the bed.

The powerful knocking eventually ceased, but later on, as the man's corpse was being removed from the hotel, a light, sharp, rapping noise seemed to accompany the procession.

It is said that the man was never identified and that the possessed room was never again rented out. Eventually, folklore has it, the hotel was torn down to make way for the post office.

End of story? Not quite. *The Encyclopedia of Ghosts and Spirits* offers this tantalizing conclusion:

Interestingly enough, stories were in circulation as recently as 1998 that the Canada Post building was haunted. In that year it was reported that strange, unexplained knocking noises were heard by postal workers on one of the upper stories.

Just another fascinating tale about things that go bump in the night…

Fort Garry Hotel

In 1995 the managing partner of the Fort Garry Hotel, Ida Albo, was touring the old building's catacomb-like sub-basement with a reporter from the *Winnipeg Free Press.* In reference to the dark and eerie atmosphere, Albo laughingly said, "We often joke there's got to be someone buried down here."

No one has discovered a corpse, as of yet. But the dead do take up a certain amount of space at the grand, old hotel. For as many people know, the Fort Garry—like any building worth its National Historic Site papers—is haunted. Throughout the years, there have been many ghost stories told. Most are about phantoms who would appear to be reliving the wonderful times they enjoyed at the hotel. No one can blame them for wanting to do so—for the early days at the Fort Garry were glorious days indeed.

Everyone in Winnipeg had been impressed by the massive, limestone structure with the steep, chateau-style copper roof that had become a mainstay of "important"

Canadian architecture. The Grand Trunk Pacific Railway's newest hotel stood like a castle in the midst of the prairie city, close to both the Manitoba Legislative buildings and the gate of the Hudson's Bay Company post from which it took its name. It was a first-class establishment, one the *Winnipeg Free Press* compared to the Parthenon in Athens. At the opening-night gala, the province's lieutenant-governor announced, "In a building such as this we cannot claim any longer to be pioneers."

Naturally, the grand opening was a world-class affair. December 10, 1913, might have been a cold winter night, but the weather could not dampen the excitement of Winnipeg's elite social set as the hotel opened its doors. The next day, the *Free Press* required two pages of painstaking detail to describe what was headlined as a "Function of Great Brilliancy." The richness of the decor, the magnificence of the airy public spaces, the splendor of the sculptures and chandeliers—it was all deemed to be beautiful to an extent "which words [could] only describe very inadequately." The reporter did manage to find the words to describe "a few" of the ball gowns worn by the ladies in attendance—"a few" being in the neighborhood of more than one hundred.

"Mrs. Mathers, lovely gown of flame-colored chiffon velour, the bodice of silver lace with diamante embroidery and finished with a butterfly bow of black tulle...Mrs. R. H. Le Roy, pale pink satin bordered with white ostrich...Miss Ashdown, gold satin trimmed with sequined chiffon bordered with fur...Mrs. William Robinson, Madonna-blue chiffon embroidered in blue and gold draped with white satin..." The paper went on in vivid detail and announced that the scene in the ballroom had been "one of rare beauty—[an] event [that] will long be remembered."

And, some believe, it was an event that was also destined to long be relived.

The effusive descriptions of the ball gowns on that bygone magical evening are brought to mind by one of the Fort Garry Hotel's ghost stories. The tale was told to writer Gordon Sinclair, Jr., for an article in the August 8, 1995, *Winnipeg Free Press.*

The assistant manager, Don Klassen, told Sinclair about a particular woman who had stayed at the hotel on several occasions. When she arrived for one of her visits, she requested her usual room. Klassen told her that, though she was welcome to that room, he was able to offer her another that had a much more pleasing view.

"No," the woman said. "I prefer this room. The spirits visit me there."

Klassen asked the woman to elaborate, and she did quite willingly.

"There's a lady in a ball gown," she explained, "who hovers at the foot of my bed and after that, she moves out the window."

It's easy to imagine that one of the celebrants of that cold December evening has chosen to spend eternity at the Fort Garry, finding endless enjoyment in that glittering affair. It would be interesting to have a more specific description of the ghost's gown, to compare against the list that was published in the *Free Press.* By virtue of an eye-catching design or a unique shade of satin, one might be able to put a name to the spectral face.

Though Don Klassen was very interested in what the woman told him, he may have been less than surprised. There had been other reports of strange occurrences in the

The historic Fort Garry Hotel in Winnipeg, Manitoba

hotel, ranging from eerie moaning sounds to sightings of a phantom light that roamed the building's elegant hallways. And then there was the time in 1989 when Klassen was working on an audit at four o'clock in the morning. He was pulled away from his paperwork when one of the night dishwashers came running into his office.

"He was very frightened," Klassen said. "The word he used was 'freaked out.' "

The young man's mental state was understandable, given that he had just seen a ghost. He had been on a back stairway that led from the kitchen area to a dining room, which was then called "The Factor's Table." As he neared the top of the stairs, he began to hear muted sounds coming from the room. When the dishwasher walked through the swinging doors to investigate, he was greeted by the ghostly image of a man, seated at one of the tables with cutlery in hand, eating a meal.

"He didn't look up," Klassen later said of the apparition. "He didn't acknowledge [the dishwasher's] presence at all."

Don Klassen accompanied the unnerved employee back to the dining room. The ghost had vanished by that time, leaving no evidence of his visit and no leftovers from his meal. To be certain the whole episode was not some imaginative prank, Klassen checked all the doors leading into the dining room. All had been locked from the inside.

In the 1995 *Winnipeg Free Press* article, Managing Partner Ida Albo shared her own spooky story with Gordon Sinclair, Jr. According to Sinclair's report,

> She and her husband, Rick Bel, live in the hotel. One night they got into an argument and Ida went to bed without him. She was sleeping, face down, when she was woken by Rick entering the room. She didn't bother turning over. She didn't want to get into it again. Then she felt him sit down on the bed beside her.
>
> Finally, she turned over to talk.
>
> But Rick wasn't there.
>
> No one was there.

What a shame that Albo didn't turn over a few minutes earlier—it would be interesting to know what she would have seen. Perhaps it was a sympathetic visit from a lady in a lovely ball gown or a hungry spirit taking a detour on his way to the dining room or an orb of spectral light, hovering just over the bed covers. Or perhaps she would have seen someone or something that no one had seen before.

It wouldn't be that surprising. Nearly a century's worth of history means that there are likely many more spirits waiting to introduce themselves at the magnificent Fort Garry Hotel.

CHAPTER IV

Spirits of the South

La Posada de Santa Fe

Located in the heart of Santa Fe, New Mexico, on six beautifully landscaped acres is the oasis of serenity and rejuvenation known as La Posada de Santa Fe Resort and Spa. The 159 adobe-style suites and rooms surround a Victorian-era inn, which serves as the main facility. This historic building was not always an inn, however. It was once the family home of Abraham and Julia Staab.

Abraham Staab emigrated from Germany in the mid-1800s and established himself as a successful businessman. Once he had prospered financially, he returned to Germany to seek a bride. When he came back to America, it was with a lovely young woman named Julia Shuster. Julia made Abraham a fine wife and bore him eight children. In 1884 he built her a grand three-story house on Santa Fe's Palace Avenue. The brick, mahogany and marble were all shipped by suppliers in the East. The furnishings, artwork and statuary came directly from Europe. The home was magnificent, and Julia Staab entertained all of Santa Fe society there—when her health permitted. The woman suffered countless illnesses and had been weakened by her numerous pregnancies. Often she was too unwell to receive guests.

Julia Staab's greatest suffering came when her youngest child died in infancy. It is said that for two horrible weeks, the grief-stricken mother did not sleep. When at last she did, she awoke to find that her long, dark hair had turned prematurely white. Julia had aged beyond her years in other ways as well. She was seldom seen in public after that, and she died in 1896 at the age of 52.

The obituaries that paid tribute to Julia indicate that

La Posada de Santa Fe as it exists today

she was loved by the city of Santa Fe. That affection must have been mutual—for Julia has long appeared reluctant to leave Santa Fe and her former home.

"Oh yes, she's been wandering around for many, many years," a former manager was once quoted as saying.

A ghost tour operator added, "She has the highest contact of any ghost in Santa Fe. She makes herself quite known."

It is true: though she may have been a recluse late in her life, Julia is not shy now. There is a wealth of stories about people who have encountered her restless spirit. Sometimes she will make herself known with a sudden rush of wind, a strong burst of lilac perfume or the

Abraham Staab built the house that is the heart of La Posada de Santa Fe, but it is the spirit of his wife, Julia, that haunts it.

rhythmic rocking motion of an empty chair. Other times her presence demonstrates itself more forcefully. Guests have, on occasion, been driven from the bedroom that was once Julia's by an incessantly, inexplicably flushing toilet. Others have been surprised to see a strange, foggy form marring their holiday photos. Still others have actually witnessed her apparition, which has been known to materialize in her room at the foot of the bed.

Julia's spirit often presents itself visually. She has been described as a lovely woman with dark eyes who wears a long, black, hooded dress. Frequently, she has been seen drifting down the stairs and through the parlor of her former home. She has been known to quietly observe the staff at work as well—several employees have reported looking up from their duties to find Julia staring at them intently.

An early sketch of the Staab Mansion

It is undoubtedly the conscientious staff of La Posada who have come to know Julia best. They know that she can be exasperating—as she was the time she pulled a full tray of brimming champagne glasses from a waiter's hand. But they also know that she can be helpful—as she was the time she lit the boiler on an unexpectedly cold night when the maintenance man could not be found. Ever the concerned hostess, Julia got the heat flowing. To this day, the staff cannot explain how else it could have happened.

Just knowing that Julia could show up at any moment tends to keep the staff on their toes. A security guard's alertness was once tested when he looked into a mirror in the men's washroom and saw Julia looking back. Two other employees were guiding a group tour of the hotel when Julia thoroughly unnerved them. They had been about to enter her second-floor bedroom, which was vacant. But when they knocked briefly on the door as a matter of standard procedure, everyone present clearly heard a woman's voice reply, "I'm in here." The group waited patiently by the door while the employees went to the front desk to confirm that the room had not been rented. When they were told that no one was supposed to be occupying the room, they went in to investigate. They found the space entirely empty with the windows securely locked from the inside.

That is not the only time that Julia Staab's ghost has been known to speak. The night of the boiler incident, the front desk clerk received a call from an unidentified woman who expressed concern about the discomfort of "her guests" and assured him that she would "take care of the problem herself." And there is a woman named Brigid O'Toole who believes that Julia once spoke directly to her.

O'Toole had just moved to Santa Fe and had arranged to meet some friends at La Posada. While she waited, she "saw a lady in an outrageous tea gown." As she was thinking about how attractive the dress was, the woman who was wearing it looked directly at her.

"Thank you," she said.

That experience alone would have been strange enough. But several months later, O'Toole returned to La Posada with some friends. When they walked into the library, she noticed a portrait hanging over the mantel.

"Oh! There's the lady I saw in the tea dress!" she exclaimed.

Her friends were stunned. They told her that the woman in the portrait was Julia Staab, who had been dead for nearly a century. It was the first time Brigid O'Toole had ever heard about the ghost.

One question has never been satisfactorily answered: why does Julia's spirit remain earthbound? Some people simply believe that she remains in her home because she loves it; it was built to make her happy. Others say that she may be trapped here by her lifetime of physical suffering, even suggesting that she was once an "empathic person" who took on the pain of those around her. There are also darker theories, however, hinting at mental illness and mistreatment at the hands of her husband. These are likely fueled by the mysterious facts that she was never seen in her last years and her exact cause of death was never revealed. It is also known that Abraham Staab—despite being known for his benevolence in the community—was considered by his own children and grandchildren to be cruelly strict and controlling.

But no matter how unpleasant the circumstances of Julia Staab's last years may have been, she does seem to be content now. Truly there is no reason she should not be. Her beloved home is now even more beautiful than it was in her lifetime, and the current management goes to great lengths to ensure that the ghostly "lady of the house" remains happy.

"We are currently returning her bedroom to the original Victorian style," La Posada's managing director, Daniel Hostettler, recently reported. "[It is being appointed with] antiques and historically accurate colors and linens. We've also placed a leather-bound book entitled 'Julia's Ghost Stories' into the suite so that our guests can write down their experiences and pass them on..."

Given Julia's haunting habits, that book will soon be filled with intriguing tales about the beautiful, dark-eyed, spectral mistress of La Posada de Santa Fe.

The Gadsden Hotel

The Gadsden Hotel, with its five stories reaching up into the clear blue desert sky, is the tallest building in the quiet border town of Douglas, Arizona. After 95 years of hosting cattle and copper barons and with a name borrowed from the man who orchestrated the famous Gadsden Purchase, it is also Douglas' most historic building. With its white Italian marble staircase and magnificent, 42-foot, Tiffany stained-glass mural, it is arguably one of the most beautiful structures in southern Arizona. And there are few who would try to dispute the hotel's one other claim to fame. For everyone knows that the Gadsden is, without a doubt, the most haunted place in Douglas.

Hartman and Doris Brekhus knew the ghost stories, along with everything else about the hotel. The North Dakota couple spent their annual winter vacations at the Gadsden for decades. They liked the people and the town and found it difficult to stand by and watch as the hotel began to decline. So in 1988 they bought it. They installed their daughter-in-law, Robin Brekhus, as hotel manager and began using any profits to restore the historic building.

Robin Brekhus had never managed a hotel before—but that didn't stop her from doing it. She had no prior experiences with ghosts, either, but that didn't keep her from meeting one in the hotel's labyrinth of a basement on March 13, 1991.

On the afternoon of that day, the hotel suffered a power outage. Robin Brekhus immediately grabbed a flashlight and ran down to the basement room where she kept a box of battery-operated candles.

"Suddenly," Brekhus recalled, "I got the feeling that

someone was watching me. And, so, I turned around ...Nobody there. I opened the door, grabbed my box of candles, and I got this feeling again. So I turned and looked and shone my flashlight down the hall. And there—it wasn't very far away—there was this man standing there watching me. And it was like he was waiting for me to see him because, the minute I saw him, he just kind of turned and moved down the hallway. He didn't float...but he didn't really walk either. He just kind of moved down the hallway."

Brekhus wasted no time getting back upstairs. Once she was safely out of the basement, she took a moment to pull herself together. She had a hotel full of guests and no electricity—a problem that had to be dealt with immediately. She quickly resolved to take care of the urgent business first and put the ghostly encounter out of her mind until she had some time to stop and calmly think about it. When she finally got back to the front desk, however, her assistant, who had been waiting impatiently with a pile of batteries, could see that something was wrong.

"What happened to you?" the woman asked. "You look like you just saw a ghost!"

"Those were her actual words!" Brekhus later laughed. "And I said, 'I did! I saw the ghost!' All this after I had firmly told myself that I wasn't going to think about it!"

Robin Brekhus must have been unnerved, but she couldn't have been entirely surprised. Ghost stories about the hotel went back for decades and there were many employees who would go to great lengths to avoid the basement area in particular.

"Many, many years ago," she said, "employees got so

they wouldn't even go to the bathroom because they had to go down to the basement. The people who owned the hotel at the time wouldn't let the employees use the lobby bathrooms because those were for guests. So some people...they'd have to leave to go to the bathroom because they would *not* go downstairs."

Carmen Diaz, who operated the Gadsden's manual elevator for more than a quarter-century, offered a succinct description of the phantom that she saw in the hotel's basement.

"Tall man," Diaz reported. "Black pantsuit. No head."

But avoiding the basement was no guarantee that an employee would avoid the phenomena altogether. The restaurant supervisor, a woman named Brenda Maley, had a strange and frightening experience as she lay in bed in her hotel room one night. She suddenly became aware that she was unable to move. On the wall she was facing, she could see the shadow of her own body and the shadow of another form menacingly hunched over her.

There was another woman—a hotel guest—who also had a ghost join her in bed. (The two incidents inspired a tabloid writer to pen a short article with the blaring headline "SEX-MAD GHOST STALKS HOTEL—and guests are LOVING it!") But while Maley had described her experience as being distressing, the guest had a more positive reaction.

"This lady was staying here in room 333," Robin Brekhus recalled. "She was nice, kind of prim and proper-looking, in town doing research on her family history. So after she was here for two or three nights, she came up to the desk and asked for me. So they came and got me out of the restaurant and I said, 'Yes ma'am,' figuring she had a problem with her room or something. Well—she kind of did!

"She said, 'Well, I'm going to tell you something and I hope you don't think I'm odd.' "

The woman went on to explain that very early that morning in her hotel room, she had felt someone get into bed with her. Her first thought was that someone else had obtained a key to her room. But, when the woman opened her eyes, she could plainly see that the chain-lock on the door was still securely in place. She rolled over then to face whoever was in bed with her. As she did, she felt a weight lift off that side of the mattress, as though someone had left the bed.

The sun had barely begun to rise. It was much too early to get up and the woman was still tired, so she convinced herself that the whole episode had been caused by her imagination. She decided to roll over and go back to sleep.

"So she rolled over," said Brekhus, "and the minute she did, somebody got into bed with her and spooned her and put their arms around her. She said she had arms around her and a body right next to her body!"

Quite naturally, the woman was alarmed. But being of a practical nature, she decided to relax and simply enjoy the comforting sensation while she drifted off to sleep.

"I went to sleep with arms around me," she told Robin Brekhus, "and when I woke up, they were gone."

Exactly one year later, a motion picture crew was staying at the hotel while they filmed the movie *Ruby Jean and Joe.* On the night before they were to leave, one of the crew members, who had become friendly with Brekhus, accosted her as she walked into the lobby of the hotel.

"[He] grabbed me by the shirt and pulled me to his face," she said. "And he was shaking me, saying, 'Robin, why didn't you tell me you have ghosts!? The bartender says that you knew!' "

It turned out that the man had been having strange experiences all week long, and that the night before he had watched in fear as some unseen force flipped the overhead lights on and off and threw his golf bag across the hotel room.

"It wasn't like they tipped over," he stressed to Brekhus. "It was like someone grabbed the edge of the bag and just flung it across the floor. I didn't dare get up to turn on the TV or turn off the lights. I just lay there all night. I didn't sleep another wink."

When Brekhus asked the fellow what room he was in, he told her "room 333." It was the same room where the woman had been "spooned" by a spectral visitor. Brekhus later laughed about it.

"Whatever's in there definitely prefers the female guests," she noted.

Though several ghostly incidents have taken place on the third floor, Brekhus insists that the activity is not especially concentrated there. To illustrate her point, she rattled off a number of paranormal experiences had by people on every other floor of the Gadsden Hotel.

There has been an apparition of a man seen on the mezzanine, which overlooks the lobby. The cooks have seen knives float across the kitchen. On the fourth floor, one of the maids ("a real no-nonsense type of woman," according to Brekhus) frequently hears her name being called by a ghostly voice. Two women guests saw "a man who wasn't there" near the second-floor coin-operated laundry. They ran to spend the night in a nearby motel, despite Robin's assurances that none of the Gadsden's ghosts had ever hurt anyone. There have been countless supernatural occurrences in Robin Brekhus' office as well and in the suite that she shares with her husband and children. And, of course, there have been the many eerie things that have taken place in the basement.

One of the most intriguing basement incidents took place in the mid-1990s, when the television program *Sightings* taped an episode at the Gadsden.

Psychic Peter James had been contracted to take part in the production, but had been told nothing about the hotel or even where he was going. On the afternoon when he first walked into the hotel, he had never been there or spoken with Robin Brekhus before.

The TV crew had been at the Gadsden several days in advance of James' arrival. They had been taping interviews and dramatically recreating Brekhus' first encounter with the ghost. They had just completed the recreation when James got to the hotel. The psychic was brought down to the basement to meet everyone involved in the shoot. He was introduced to Robin Brekhus, who offered him her hand. Instead of shaking it, though, James suddenly turned and walked right past her.

"He said, 'Do you guys know that there's somebody here watching you right now?' " Brekhus recalled. "And then he described the ghost and it was exactly what I had just described on camera. And there's no way he could have known. No way."

It was incredible enough that James was seeing exactly what Robin Brekhus had seen years before. But even more astounding, James walked down the dark hall and stopped in the exact spot where Brekhus had seen the ghost.

"He's right here," Peter James said.

• • •

The Gadsden, like all hotels of its age, has recorded a few on-premises deaths. Brekhus isn't aware of any violent deaths in the building, though, and says that no lives were lost in a fire that all but destroyed the hotel in 1928. Some would think it rather strange that, despite this notable lack of tragedy, the Gadsden is so obviously and actively haunted. Who are these spirits, and why have they chosen to remain at the hotel?

Of course no one knows for sure, but Peter James did share some of his impressions with Robin Brekhus.

"He feels that three of the spirits are here because they're trapped in a love triangle," she said. "There are two men and a woman named Annie. The men are here because Annie is; neither one wants to leave and let the other one have her."

So some of the ghosts are there because they love "Annie," while others undoubtedly remain simply because they love the Gadsden Hotel. It's understandable. This self-professed "last of the grand hotels," steeped in atmosphere and history, would be quite a wonderful place to spend eternity.

Crescent Hotel

The quaint Ozark Mountains town of Eureka Springs, Arkansas, is known by many different names. It has been called "the city that water built" because of the seemingly endless number of freshwater springs that drew people to the area. It is often referred to as "America's Victorian Village" because of the abundance of charming 19th-century architecture. And it has been called haunted. Many people believe that Eureka Springs is more populated by the dead than it is by the living—perhaps because so many people died of their various ailments after traveling to the area in search of a mineral water cure.

In this very haunted town, few will argue that the most haunted location is the massive gothic limestone mansion that overlooks it. She is "The Grand Old Lady of the Ozarks," the legendary Crescent Hotel. No one at the hotel will dispute its supernatural reputation. The staff have, in past advertising, referred to themselves as "The Ozark Mountains Center of Paranormal Activity."

The Crescent Hotel was built from 1884 to 1886 by the Eureka Springs Improvement Company—a corporation organized some years earlier in an effort to improve the shanty-town conditions that met those who traveled great distances to take advantage of the healing springs and fresh mountain air. It was an impressive structure, deemed by the local newspaper to be "the most important work done in the city so far." Interestingly, by the time those words were written in 1885, the hotel was likely already home to its first spectral guest.

The great limestone blocks that form the walls of the Crescent Hotel were hand-cut during construction by a crew of Irish stonemasons. One of the young men on the crew, a fellow named Michael, fell to his death during the project. He either fell *from* the second floor or landed *on* the second floor (accounts vary), but room 218 has been haunted by his presence ever since.

Some guests in that room have looked into the mirror and have been startled to see Michael looking back. Once, a salesman staying in the room reported that "someone or something" had tried to push him out of bed. Over the years, several people have been victims of the ghost's repertoire of tricks. Generally, Michael's pranks are of the harmless variety—although one, reported by Richard D. Seifried in the May 2000 issue of *FATE* magazine, was rather gruesome. Seifried claimed that the guest in question had awakened to find that he had been sleeping in a large pool of blood. At first the man thought he had cut himself, but a thorough examination showed that he had no wound. Usually Michael makes himself known in a less gory fashion, however, and room 218 has become very popular among guests.

Eureka Springs and the Crescent Hotel enjoyed several years of economic boom. Then, just prior to World War I, something changed. People began to realize that there were no miracle cures to be had in the bubbling Ozarks water and business slowed considerably. Though the springs continued to gush, tourism slowed to a trickle. Economic hardship forced the Crescent Hotel to reinvent itself as the "Crescent College and Conservatory for Young Women." For many years, the girls' boarding school provided a perfect remedy for the hotel's problem of nearly non-existent winter tourism. During the summer, the Crescent was still a reasonably busy resort hotel, but from

September through May wealthy families from across the country paid an exorbitant 400 dollars per year to have their daughters educated there.

There are stories, however, that this era in the Crescent's history was marked by another tragedy. Some say that a girl either fell or was pushed to her death from the fourth-floor observation porch. Ever since, the teen's phantom has been seen wandering through the lush, green gardens that surround the hotel.

The Crescent College and Conservatory for Young Women was one of many small, private schools that fell victim to the Great Depression. It closed its doors at the end of the 1933 college year. The four or five years that followed were a sad time for the "Grand Old Lady of the Ozarks." The hotel was leased and operated by a variety of people, and much of the fine furniture was sold to guests at bargain prices just to make ends meet. Finally in 1937, the hotel closed because of financial strain and a general lack of interest. It looked like the end of an era—but, in fact, it was the beginning of a strange, new one.

Dr. Norman Baker called himself a champion for "medical freedom." His detractors called him a fraud. The people of Eureka Springs were likely unsure of the true story when Baker bought the Crescent Hotel and turned it into his own private cancer clinic. They only knew that there were huge changes taking place.

Baker spent a reported 50,000 dollars remodeling the Victorian structure to suit his needs. Ugly concrete sun porches were added, interior doors were removed and the walls were painted in various shades of the doctor's favorite color, purple. Once renovations were complete, "Baker Hospital" was advertised far and wide. Dr. Baker's pamphlets promised that he could both cure people of cancer and free them from "the medical octopus," as he called organized medicine. Eventually it was the eccentric doctor's advertising that did him in. In 1940 he was found guilty of using the mail to defraud with his alleged cancer cures. Norman Baker went to prison for four years, but not before untold numbers had died while in his care.

The Crescent stood dark and silent from 1940 until 1946. It was purchased then by four business partners who undid the damage of Norman Baker's remodeling; they restored the building to its former, grand state. It was a massive undertaking, but one worth the effort, for since that time, the Crescent Hotel has operated as the luxurious and elegant resort it was originally intended to be. For a time, it was promoted as a "Castle in the Air, High Atop the Ozarks." In his book *The Grand Old Lady of the Ozarks* (Eagles' Nest Press, 1986), Dr. D. R. Woolery asked, "Whoever heard of a castle without ghosts?" Indeed, during the 1970s it became apparent that the Crescent was indeed haunted by her colorful past.

Woolery wrote about an experience one of the hotel's owners had in 1973:

> [He] was in the hotel's lobby and saw a man, dressed turn-of-the-century style, all in black with a frock coat and white shirt, standing by the staircase. He wore a moustache and his face was accentuated by an unnatural pallor. As [the owner] stared at this perfect replica of a man, the apparition seemed to evaporate into thin air…

The following year, the same owner was wakened out of a sound sleep to witness yet another apparition:

> ...[He] found himself face-to-face with a strange luminescent figure standing at the foot of his bed. The form was that of an older man with a moustache and beard, who seemed to be composed of a myriad of radiant filaments suspended in the profound darkness...

Several different phantoms have been seen at the Crescent Hotel over the last three decades. There is the specter of a nurse, undoubtedly from Dr. Baker's day, who has been seen pushing a gurney down a hallway. A Native American man is said to haunt the fourth floor. In the dining room there is a ghost who often materializes at one particular table—whether or not it is occupied by other guests. It is also rumored that on rare occasions one can catch a fleeting glimpse of the past as the room becomes momentarily filled with Victorian-era diners.

The North Penthouse—once Dr. Baker's residence—seems particularly active. In his *FATE* magazine article, Richard D. Seifried wrote:

> During the winter of 1998, some guests met in the North Penthouse to plan for a wedding. Forty-five ghosts showed up. The room was so crowded that the living visitors left. Someone returned, negotiations took place and finally most of the spirits left. One disgruntled ghost materialized in a lady's car after the wedding.

One Crescent entity, named "Theodora" by the staff, stays strictly in room 419. She is said to have a sweet disposition unless a guest makes some complaint about the accommodations. Anyone who dares to do that can expect to find their luggage piled in front of the door. It is Theodora's unmistakable invitation to leave.

Today the Crescent Hotel wholeheartedly embraces its past—including its ghosts. Anyone searching for a spectral encounter stands a good chance of having one within the historic walls of this "Grand Old Lady of the Ozarks."

Hotel Vendome

This is the ghost's story:

Her name was Abby Byr. She and her husband owned the Hotel Vendome in Prescott, Arizona, in its early years. The Byrs eventually lost the hotel for unpaid taxes but were fortunate in that the new owners retained them as managers and allowed them to live in room 16. Perhaps the owners didn't have the heart to evict the couple, as Abby was severely ill. She had "consumption," they say, and was wasting away by degrees. One day in 1921 she sent her husband out to fetch some medicine. Mr. Byr left—and never returned. This abandonment was Abby's final undoing. She took to her bed, refused to eat or drink and died at the young age of 33. Her faithful cat, Noble, perished by Abby's side. Their spirits have remained in room 16 ever since.

This tale is part legend, part assumption and part information gathered in a séance in 1986. The haunting,

Hotel Vendome in Prescott, Arizona, home to the spirits of Abby Byr and her faithful cat, Noble

however, is a matter of fact—proven by the seemingly endless experiences of both staff and guests over many years. It is one of the best-documented ghost stories in Arizona, subject of countless paranormal investigations, newspaper articles and television reports. Among ghost-hunting enthusiasts, Abby's celebrity may be unmatched.

The Hotel Vendome has long been popular because of its genteel western atmosphere. The 21-room inn was lovingly restored in the early 1980s and boasts such charming features as a sweeping front veranda, original wood transoms and an inviting lobby wine bar. Abby, the resident ghost, only adds to the Vendome's historic appeal. Her popularity stems from the fact that she is a particularly active spirit who seldom disappoints those who come to visit her.

Abby's repertoire of tricks is extensive. The radiators often rattle and wheeze, although they were disconnected several years ago in favor of a new heating and cooling system. Guests in room 16—known as "Abby's Room"—

sometimes find that they have no hot water, which is mysterious because the entire hotel is on the same plumbing system. Objects sometimes move about, strong perfume sometimes permeates the air and it is not uncommon to be chilled by a sudden, icy breeze on the hottest of afternoons. There are days when the smoke alarm beeps intermittently and times when the television sound won't work for anything except a western film. And guests will often hear the meowing of a cat and sense that there is "something strange" about the closet—even when they don't know that it is where the unfortunate feline is believed to have died.

Despite being this busy in room 16, Abby's spirit still finds time to wander through the rest of the hotel. She once indicated, through a Ouija board, that she was free to roam throughout the Vendome—and a trail of paranormal phenomena supports this.

"People have seen her roaming the staircase and the hallways," said former owner Rama Patel. "They've even seen her in other rooms. Also, there's a service bell on the front desk, so guests can ring for service; you'll hear it when there's nobody there. And sometimes you'll hear the doorbell ring, but there's nobody in the lobby."

A former employee, Michaela Dixon, experienced something far more personal than a game of ghostly "knock on ginger." It happened one night when there were no guests and no other staff to keep her company.

"It was just myself, here in the hotel," she recalled. "I went down to the cellar and started doing the beer inventory—and I felt a hand on my shoulder. I literally fell off the stool, threw the folder down on the floor and thought *That's it! I'm not doing any more inventory!* I ran up the stairs and, all the time, I felt like someone was right behind me."

Though Dixon had never believed the ghost stories before, Abby's icy touch changed her mind.

"Before then, I was very, very much a disbeliever," she said, "but then she gave me a reason to believe."

Those who need such convincing usually receive it when they visit the Vendome. Abby seems to be an exceptionally strong spirit, quite capable of making herself known. Dixon recalled several guests who had been taken aback by the ghost's antics.

"One guest said that he put his keys down on his bedside table and when he got up to walk to the bathroom, they hit him in the back," she said. "Just like someone had picked them up and thrown them at him. Then a lady had her watch thrown into her room when she hadn't even realized that she had lost it. She said her door opened and her watch flew through the doorway!"

In April 2001, on Friday the 13th, Abby made her presence felt once more. At exactly 3 AM, four women who were sharing a suite were awakened by the powerful scent of roses. The Vendome's owners, Frank and Kathie Langford, later learned that, at the exact same moment, another guest had an unsettling experience in the hallway outside the women's room. He was walking along when he noticed that his shadow was not moving in sync with his body.

"He froze in his tracks," reported Kathie Langford, "and the shadow moved on down the hall." She added that while the women guests had known about Abby, the man had never heard the story before.

Most people who meet Abby are more charmed by her

than spooked. There is a story going back a number of years about a couple who checked into room 16 and put a vase of fresh flowers on one side of the dresser. The couple then left the room for a short time, and when they returned, the flowers had been moved to the opposite side of the dresser. The couple moved the vase back to its original position and went to sleep. The next morning, the flowers had moved once again.

That afternoon, the wife left her husband alone in the room for a while. The man happened to look out the window at one point and saw a woman waving cheerfully at him. He waved back—then suddenly remembered that the room was on the second floor. Logically, there couldn't be a woman "just walking by" the window. He jumped up, ran outside and tried to find the woman. Of course, there was no one there.

Paranormal investigator Bill Everist, who related the story, said that the couple weren't at all frightened by their experience.

"In fact," he said, "they keep going back and staying in the same room and bringing her flowers."

Abby seems to appreciate such gifts. Michaela Dixon remembered one couple who "brought some cookies for Abby...and some food and a cat toy for Noble." They spent a peaceful night in room 16, with no radiator noise and no lack of hot water. The people who had stayed in the room the previous night provided no such offerings and had experienced a number of irritating problems.

Frank and Kathie Langford have owned the Hotel Vendome since December 2000. It wasn't long after they made their purchase that Abby introduced herself.

"It was about two weeks after we moved into the

hotel," Kathie Langford recalled. "I was behind the bar, telling my friends that I didn't believe in the whole 'Abby thing,' as I called it. As soon as the words came out of my mouth, my clock chimed. I have had that clock for over 10 years and have never been able to make it chime. It chimed several times after that when I was talking about Abby or telling the story to a customer.

"It hasn't chimed in over a year now," Kathie noted, "but I also never say such things at the bar [anymore]!"

Frank Langford tends to be less skeptical than his wife concerning matters of the paranormal. Still, he's been shaken by several of the experiences that he's had at his hotel.

"Frank says a plant fell over before his eyes, for no reason," said Kathie. "A big plant that sat firmly in the hall, on the floor. He said when he went to pick it up, a cold breeze blew over him."

Not surprisingly, Frank Langford decided that cleaning up could wait. He left the spilled plant in the hallway until later that day.

The Langfords have also discovered that the doors to both room 16 and its closet have a tendency to close by themselves.

"Probably the tilt of the building," Kathie notes dryly, although she seems to be suggesting otherwise. She does admit that the unusual events at the hotel have given her pause for thought.

"The hotel has had a very long history since [it was built in] 1917 and has seen its dark days. Although it's now bright, pleasant and very charming, many people have come in to tell us that they remember the days when it…was run down."

Did those years of dark atmosphere magnify Abby's presence somehow? Kathie Langford, once an avowed skeptic, now admits that there's "lots of stuff to ponder..."

And lots of reasons for ghost enthusiasts to visit the very paranormally active Hotel Vendome.

Goldfield Hotel

The well-preserved, semi-ghost city of Goldfield, Nevada, 182 miles northwest of Las Vegas, has been described as being "as rich in history as it once was in gold." That's a bold statement, for Goldfield was once the wealthiest of Nevada's mining towns, producing upwards of 10,000 dollars per day. Of course, that was back at the height of the boom, when the city boasted five banks, three newspapers and more than 20,000 citizens. Then, somewhere along the line, the boom went bust. Today, Goldfield's census hovers somewhere around 500. Nearly the entire population could be seated in the dining room and bar of the old Goldfield Hotel, had it not died along with most of the town.

When the Goldfield Hotel first opened its doors in 1908, it was impressive by any standards. The four-story brick structure was known as the "gem of the desert." It was adorned with marble, mahogany and hand-laid mosaic tile. Twenty-two carat gold leaf decorated the ceilings. It had the first electric elevator west of the Mississippi and a telephone in every room. But despite its opulence, the Goldfield Hotel withered along with the town of Goldfield and hasn't seen a guest since the end of World War II.

Of course, that's not to say that it's not occupied...

The hotel is widely believed to be populated by a number of spirits. Numerous psychics who have toured the dusty, old building say that it's one of only seven "portals to the other side" that exist in this world.

Goldfield resident and businesswoman Virginia Ridgway has often played the part of tour guide to such visitors. As a result, she's had some strange, unsettling experiences in the hotel. On one occasion, she was leading the town's deputy sheriff and three other people through the dark hallways when she saw one of the spectral guests.

"We just got up to the third floor," Ridgway recalled, "and at the end of the hall...we saw smoke billowing. I started to turn around and run down the stairs to call for the fire engine, but the deputy sheriff grabbed me and said, 'Wait a minute!' So I turned back around, and the smoke had dissipated and there was a figure standing there...We all saw it. It was a man leaning against the wall. He was in black western attire with a black hat...And he had an iridescent glow all the way around him."

Some time later, a television crew that had spoken with Ridgway made a plan to capture the image of the cowboy on video.

"They set the camera on the third floor, pointing to the area where my apparition appeared," said Ridgway. "And then they slept downstairs...The next morning, [they found] that somebody had turned that camera off about 10 minutes after they turned it on. But nobody had gone back up there."

Ridgway wasn't surprised. Cameras and flash bulbs

frequently malfunction inside the Goldfield Hotel, as though the ghosts are shy about having their pictures taken. The one exception was the time a reporter from the *Las Vegas Sun* snapped a picture in a small room on the first floor which showed an eerie image of a woman with flowing hair. There were those who debunked the photo, but the phantom captured on film did seem to be consistent with the description of a spirit seen by many psychics in that same room. It is believed that the young woman's name was Elizabeth and that she was a prostitute who had been confined to the room while pregnant. She was either killed or left to die there after giving birth. The baby was taken from her and thrown down the abandoned mine shaft that exists in the basement.

If this terrible tale seems too dramatic to believe, consider the fact that nearly every psychic who has ever toured the hotel has produced a story with the same details. And, according to Ridgway, they've all been credible mediums who have gone in without prior knowledge of the legend.

"All of the for-real psychics," she said, "you don't tell them anything. You just take them in. And they'll all stop at this same room and describe this same thing. They see a young girl with long hair, chained to the radiator…and there's a little bed over in the corner. And they *all* describe this, including one lady from Italy! She didn't know anything about the hotel or the town; she was just here because her car broke down. So I took her in, and when she got to the haunted room, she started screaming and ran out of there."

There seem to be other entities in the hotel along with the ghost of Elizabeth. An investigation conducted by the

Las Vegas Institute of Parapsychology found the spirits of two young children and a hotel employee near the main staircase. A "highly menacing and extremely powerful presence" was also reported in the office that was once occupied by the owner, a mining magnate named George Wingfield. There are those who believe that Wingfield was a dangerous character who would likely have been responsible for Elizabeth's imprisonment and death.

Although no one can know that with certainty, Virginia Ridgway *does* know that there's an aggressive entity in the hotel. She was once attacked by it.

"There were three of us in the back areas, snooping around for [ghosts]," she recalled. "I was just leaning against a wall when I was picked up and slammed against the wall. Just picked up—I'd say two or three inches—and pushed back...The next morning when I got up, I had a black bruise about the size of a quarter on the sole of my foot and a matching bruise on the back of my leg, just below the knee. Just like a lightning bolt had gone through it."

The experience left Ridgway wary, but not frightened.

"Most of them leave you alone," she said.

Ridgway and her psychic guests have not been the only ones to encounter the many phantoms of the Goldfield Hotel. Ridgway owns an antique and gift shop across the street from the hotel. Often her customers leave their children playing outside while they shop. On numerous occasions, those children have reported activity in the vacant hotel.

"The kids would say 'Mama, there's somebody looking at us out of that second-floor window,' " said Ridgway. "And it was always the same window."

During a major renovation in the late 1980s, the construction superintendent was once working alone, late at night, when he looked up and saw the very clear image of a crowd of spectral party-goers filling the bar. The superintendent didn't know it at the time, but those ghosts were the only guests destined to celebrate in the hotel. When the renovations were 80 percent complete, the project went bankrupt.

Indeed, it would seem that after more than half a century of being home to the dead, the Goldfield Hotel is reluctant to host the living. There have been various attempts to resurrect the old building but, according to one local man quoted in the *Las Vegas Review-Journal*, "Each owner had a little less money than the last one."

That seemed to change in 1988, when some San Francisco investors poured an estimated 4 million dollars into refurbishing the hotel. Their hope was to preserve history for "fun and profit." As it turned out, there wasn't much of either. By June 2000, the abandoned building was being auctioned for delinquent taxes.

The minimum bid was set at $426,760.26—seemingly a bargain. But perhaps it was not. The ghosts have inhabited the Goldfield Hotel for much longer than the living ever did. It seems now that they have claimed it for their own and are reluctant to let anyone, at any price, claim their afterworld home.

Oliver House

Oliver House Bed and Breakfast is nestled among the trees in the middle of the historic mining town of Bisbee, Arizona. To reach it, guests have to walk over a footbridge, crossing a water drainage system locals refer to as "the moat."

It seems fitting that Oliver House should have a moat. It is as infested with ghosts as any self-respecting European castle.

Owner Dennis Schranz was warned about the entities when he bought the place in 1986. He didn't let that stop him, however. He knew that the house—originally a boarding house and executive planning center for the Arizona and Calumet Mining Company—had an extraordinarily violent history, but he didn't believe in ghosts. So he signed the papers, took the keys and spent his first night in the historic building.

By the following day, he *did* believe in ghosts.

On that first nerve-wracking night, Schranz listened as heavy footfalls made their way down the hall, through the locked door of his room and up to the side of his bed. It was the new owner's first paranormal experience in Oliver House. It was far from his last.

"We've had this kind of stuff going on ever since," Schranz said, more than 15 years after that night. In that time, guests and staff have frequently reported voices, apparitions and chilling spectral touches. Early on, Schranz decided that he would be open about his haunting, even "before anybody else was talking about ghosts and spirits in their places."

According to him, some businesses have boasted ghost

stories that have been completely fabricated. But not Oliver House.

"We have real experiences here," he said.

Not that you have to simply take his word for it. The phenomena within the house have been extensively studied over recent years, with much of the work being done by parapsychologist Bill Everist of Pima Community College. Schranz said that in August 2001, the college submitted a report on Oliver House to an international conference on the paranormal in Freiburg, Germany. One of the immediate results was an increase in international business for the haunted bed and breakfast.

"I've had people here from [all over the world]," said Schranz, "and they all tell me that when they're here, they get the highest readings ever on their equipment."

That information would likely not surprise Bill Everist. He once conducted a field experiment at the house that yielded fascinating—and rather unexpected—results.

In 1992 Everist took a large group of people on an overnight excursion to Oliver House. He would later write, "The investigation team consisted of 19 student sensitives, two local residents and two professional psychics. None of them was given any information about the building's history."

Everist purposely kept his participants uninformed. He wanted to see if members of the group, who knew nothing of the ghost stories associated with Oliver House, would independently report impressions that were similar to one another's, or similar to experiences that had been reported in the house in the past.

Everist expected to discover some interesting correlations. He also expected to hear reports of many sounds and sensations that could be easily explained away in the light of morning. But he did not expect to hear what the participants told him over breakfast.

Everist explained his findings to Loyd Auerbach in the October 1995 issue of *FATE* magazine:

> The following morning, in a formal discussion of the evening's events, members of the investigation party revealed unusual dream experiences similar to an out-of-body experience or to lucid dreams. Participants indicated that they were awake in their dream and experiencing a foreign presence uncommon in the current time frame.

In other words, a large number of the people dreamed that they saw ghosts in their rooms, or dreamed that they had risen from their beds and walked through the darkened hallways of Oliver House in search of spirits.

Some of the journal entries were intriguing.

"I dreamed I woke up from [another] dream and saw the clothes rack on the other side of the room," wrote one woman. "To the left of the clothes rack, I felt a presence. The presence was just watching us sleep."

A man wrote, "I sat up in bed (in my dream) and looked in a mirror, which reflected the image of a young woman with...short brown hair." In the same dream, the second time the man looked, he saw "a different woman—about the same age, but with longer dark hair."

One participant later commented, "I don't normally remember my dreams, but these dreams were different. I was much more aware. The vividness was outstanding."

Could the students have experienced a sort of "dream

haunting?" It would seem that anything is possible in this strange house.

Dennis Schranz remembers that night well. He later offered a number of colorful details that may not otherwise have been recorded in the objective course of scientific study.

"It was a bright, sunny, beautiful day," said Schranz, "and as soon as [Bill Everist] and his group got here, the weather changed. Just as people finished crossing the bridge to our place, the sky turned kind of yellowish and the wind started blowing icy cold. We had a hailstorm and a rainstorm that forced the whole group into the building."

An hour later, the house directly opposite Oliver House burned to the ground. But it was not the end of the excitement.

"They had a person from a TV station in Tucson here," Schranz said. "She wasn't participating and it was clear from her body language that she thought these people were a bunch of crazies. Anyway, she stayed in the room that my assistant used to use.

"Well, the next morning Bill wanted me to tell some stories about the house. But I was handling things alone here, and there were so many people, so I said, 'Why don't I just put on the [video] tape of my assistant?' She had died a few years earlier, but we had this tape of her talking about the house.

"We put that tape on. The woman from the TV station was sitting in the audience and I saw her nudge her friend when the tape started. Then they started pointing at the TV set. Then, as the close-up [on my late assistant] came in, this lady stood up and yelled 'That's her!' "

Once the woman had calmed down, she explained why she was upset.

"What happened," said Schranz, "was that the woman was feeling a little bit uncomfortable being by herself [the night before], so she'd asked another woman to join her in her room. After half an hour or so, the two of them decided that it would be nice to have a third person join them, so they pulled in this third woman, who was passing by in the hall. They all sat up talking until six o'clock in the morning and then they all went to bed."

When the television reporter saw Schranz's assistant, who had been dead for several years, she identified her as the third woman who had been in her room until sunrise.

"Needless to say," said Schranz, "that lady has not been back."

Fortunately, most people feel differently. Many come to Oliver House specifically for the ghosts, which Dennis Schranz has never minded.

"I think it's fun," he said. "It's my fun topic. And we have people here from all over...from Britain and Argentina and Newfoundland and all these places. And what happens is, these folks sit in our parlor area and we talk about it...And we find that this is not just our experience here, but that people from all over the world have had these experiences."

Of course, most people have not experienced the paranormal to the degree with which it exists in Oliver House. But then most people don't live in a place with Oliver House's dark history.

"I have to tell you," Schranz said, "we have a post office box number, not a street address. There is no street; they dug it up and put in the water drainage system—'the moat.' But when there was a street, its name was 'Souls Avenue.' Our address, when we had one, was '26 Souls.' And we've had 26 murders take place here."

...Which may explain why there are a few restless spirits roaming the historic halls of Oliver House...

The Biltmore Hotel

When the Biltmore Hotel in Coral Gables, Florida, celebrated its 1926 grand opening, one of the celebrants, Dr. Frank Crane, made a prediction. "Many people will come and go," he said, "but this structure will remain a thing of lasting beauty."

It is evident today that Dr. Crane was right. Many people—and many eras—have come and gone at the Biltmore, yet more than 75 years after that gala opening, the Biltmore remains one of the most elegant and luxurious hotels in the world. It is as magnificent today as it was in its heyday, when it was the favorite playground of European and Hollywood royalty. In those glittering days, the Biltmore frequently registered such well-known names as the Duke and Duchess of Windsor, Ginger Rogers, Judy Garland and Bing Crosby. There were the notorious guests as well—Al Capone chief among them—who loved to relax and entertain at the Biltmore. And, according to Stephanie Kirby, who was the hotel's director of public relations in 1997, Capone was not the only underworld figure known to visit. There was another 1920s-era gangster who frequented the hotel and may have chosen to stay on in a rather permanent fashion.

The luxurious Biltmore Hotel in Coral Gables, Florida

"We have a suite here in the hotel called the 'Everglades Suite,'" Kirby explained. "It's up on the 13th floor of the tower. The Biltmore's tower is a replica of the Giralda Tower in Seville, Spain. And each floor of the tower is a very magnificent signature suite, with several bedrooms and bathrooms and private elevator access. Now the Everglades Suite is also known as the 'Al Capone Suite' because he used to frequent it back in the 1920s.

"Back in the early days, in the '20s, this suite was also used as a little mini casino. During the days of Prohibition, they used to have little gangster parties with ladies and diamonds and jewels—and, obviously, booze, which was illegal—and gambling. And many of these gangsters who were around the Miami area during the '20s would have these big parties up in the Everglades Suite.

"At one such party...there was an individual named Fats Walsh. He was a gangster—I guess a hit man—for one of the big-name gangsters. And at this party, he got into an argument with another gangster. Supposedly, when he turned to walk away, the other gangster shot him in the back. He fell in front of the big coral rock fireplace. Now there was a bookcase, supposedly, that revolved to open up a secret passageway [that led] down the fire escape. It's said that all the guests in the suite...cleared out of the room down this back fire escape. They left no evidence in the room except this body, with a sheet covering it in front of the fireplace.

"Because they never found the murderer—they never convicted anyone of it or sent anyone to jail for it—it is said that his spirit lingers in the Everglades Suite. And he's never been able to rest in peace, because his murder was never avenged."

Kirby went on to explain that the gangster's "lingering spirit" had never caused any problems at the Biltmore.

"He was a fairly jolly-type person with a good disposition, they say," she stressed. "So it follows that his spirit is quite friendly. But sometimes, they say, he gets lonely. So when a guest gets into the tower elevator, [it'll pass the guest's floor] and just go up to 13 automatically. And you have to have a private key for access above the 11th floor! But they say that it's because Fats is lonely and would like people to come visit him when there's no one in the suite."

Stephanie Kirby said that there were stories going all the way back to the 1930s of doors that would open and close by themselves in the Everglades Suite. She thought

The Biltmore Hotel's "Al Capone Suite," afterlife home of gangster Fats Walsh

the tales were fairly credible, because of their longevity.

"It's a story that has been told by many people and has remained intact over the years," she said.

The story remained intact, even during long stretches of time when it seemed that the Biltmore Hotel would not. During World War II, the War Department converted the beautiful Mediterranean-style building into a hospital. The marble floors were covered with government-issue linoleum, and many of the windows were sealed with concrete. The veterans' hospital remained through the 1960s. Then, for much of the '70s and '80s, the structure sat empty and unused. It became a target for vagrants, vandals and rumors.

"It was abandoned for so many years," recalled Stephanie Kirby. "It was boarded up, with 'no trespassing' signs, and a lot of teenagers in the area would try to break in. Especially on Halloween night. It had always given this impression of being like an old haunted house because it was left abandoned and it's a big monstrosity of a resort in the middle of a residential area."

But it wasn't only teenagers who thought that the Biltmore appeared to be haunted. In the late 1970s, authors Richard Winer and Nancy Osborn investigated the then-vacant building and wrote about it in a chapter of their book *Haunted Houses* (Bantam Books, 1979).

Winer and Osborn took four psychics and two tape recorders into the Biltmore and conducted a séance, which they declared garnered astounding results. The July 18, 1979, *Palm Beach Post* quoted Winer as saying, "The mediums picked up the impression of a little old man walking around the circle with a cane. They made a point of saying the man was 'irritating [them]...' "

Nancy Osborn told the *Post*'s reporter the rest of the story.

"We took the tape home," she added, "and there was this sound—tippity tap tap, tippity tap tap." She said that only one of the recorders picked up the tapping sound.

Later that same year, the *Miami Herald* reported that a group of people that called themselves the "Science Fiction Fantasy Society" conducted a similar investigation. Their audiotape revealed a minute-long episode of spectral heavy breathing, ending in a tired sigh. In retrospect, it's easy to imagine that the sound was made by the building itself as it waited patiently for someone to restore it to its former dignity.

It was a wait that would go on until 1988, when after a full restoration, the Biltmore reopened its elegant doors. In 1992 there was another refurbishment. Gradually, through years of hard work and millions of dollars, the Biltmore began to look like itself again. It was a major achievement, which was officially recognized in 1996 when the Biltmore was awarded National Historic Landmark status.

"It is the highest recognition that can be given by the federal government," said Ellen Uguccioni, Historic Preservation Director for the City of Coral Gables. "It means the Biltmore is part of American history."

It is also a world-class hotel. If Fats Walsh or any of his spectral friends remain, they are spending eternity in the highest style.

The Driskill Hotel

Author's note:
This story was recounted in my Ghost Stories of Texas *(Lone Pine Publishing, 2001) but was such an intriguing account that I felt it belonged in this collection as well.*

It is near midnight, and there is a hush in the lushly appointed hallways of Austin's Driskill Hotel. Near the guest rooms of the top floor, an elevator door opens with a mechanical whisper and reveals that it carries no passengers. In the deserted hall, there is a movement of air, a suggestion of footsteps, a presence of personality, although no one can be seen. Then there is a pause, and the air appears to shimmer directly in front of one particular door. Moments later, inside the room, a woman is gently awakened by a gentle, flirtatious caress. In her state of twilight consciousness, it takes several seconds for her to realize that she is supposed to be alone…

The Driskill Hotel, Austin, Texas, in 1894

• • •

Austin historian Mary Starr Barkley once said, "Probably no place in the Austin area is more heaped with history than the Driskill Hotel." Few would disagree with that. From the time of the magnificent Texas hotel's opening to the present day, the Driskill has played an important part in all that has taken place in the state capital. In fact, the Driskill was significant from its moment of inception—it was to be Austin's first hotel, designed on a scale so grand and luxurious that it would draw guests from far and wide.

The man who held the original vision was a wealthy Texas cattle baron, Colonel Jesse Lincoln Driskill. In June

1884 Driskill chose a location and announced his plans to build. Two-and-a-half years later, those plans finally came to fruition, and the impressive $400,000 hotel opened to tremendous fanfare.

Three days prior to the grand opening, the *Daily Statesman* of December 17, 1886, promised its readers "an accurate description of one of the finest hotels in the whole country." It then went on to expound upon the virtues of the Driskill, employing adjectives as ornate as the architecture.

There was no doubt that the majestic brick and limestone building was impressive enough to inspire such florid language. High stone arches, elaborate carvings and splendid marble columns gave it substance and importance. The finest materials and craftsmanship made it luxurious and plush. The appointments were first class, and the technology—including a hydraulic elevator and a bell system that enabled guests to ring for assistance from the comfort of their rooms—was the most advanced of the day. The *Daily Statesman* called the Driskill "this palace hotel of the south," and all who saw it agreed.

Colonel Driskill must have been proud to give his name to such a resplendent structure. It's a good thing that he did, for while his name remained, literally carved in stone, the man himself did not. Within one year of the spectacular opening, the financially strapped colonel was forced to close his proud monument. It was the first of countless changes in ownership of the hotel. The Driskill saw three different proprietors within its first four years alone, and there would be many more to come.

Though the Driskill was known for changing hands, it was better known as the scene of many significant events in Austin's history. It was the first hotel southwest of St. Louis to feature electric lighting. In October 1898 Austin's first long-distance telephone call was placed from the lobby of the Driskill. It is even rumored that when the Texas Rangers formed the plan that would eventually stop the legendary bank robbers Bonnie and Clyde, they did so in a suite at the Driskill Hotel. These events alone would have secured a page in history for the hotel, yet they pale in comparison to the Driskill's impact in the state's political arena.

The Driskill was once perfectly described by author and history professor Joe B. Frantz as the "living room for Texas politics." Writer Davis Hanners agreed; in his December 21, 1986, *Dallas Morning News* article concerning the hotel's centennial celebration, he wrote,

> [T]he Driskill has presided over the financial and political fortunes of those who would be king and those who would be dethroned. Its rooms have played host to nervous politicians—Lyndon Johnson chief among them—who have sweated out election returns into the wee hours. Its ballrooms have been the scene of elegant inaugural balls of many of the state's governors. Its bar has long been the haunt of lobbyists eager to bend a legislator's ear over a stiff drink.

Past statesmen seemed to agree. According to former governor Price Daniel, "If you were interested in Texas government, the Driskill is where you hung out." Indeed, it was once said that if you wanted to find anyone who amounted to anything, you looked first in the Driskill lobby and then its bar.

Being the scene of such influence made the Driskill important, not only to Austinites, but to all Texans. In his 1973 book *The Driskill*, Joe B. Frantz wrote, "To the sensitive Texan there could be no peace in Valhalla unless he had spent at least one night within the Driskill before committing his body to the Lord." Frantz might have added that, for some, the Driskill held such tremendous appeal that they were choosing to stay on even after "committing" their bodies elsewhere. Somewhere along the line, people began to say that one of the most haunted buildings in Austin was the Driskill Hotel.

Over the years, stories accumulated about employees and guests who had never checked out of the Driskill. The housekeepers spoke of hearing footsteps behind them in the halls yet finding no one there when they turned to greet the person. The office telephones were known to act in strange ways. Some guests complained that their luggage was moved around their room at night as they slept. Of course, no hotel employee would have entered the room, and no rational explanation could ever be found.

The paranormal explanation that many offered over the years was that it was a haunting connected to two tragic events that had taken place at the Driskill. According to legend, a murder had been committed in one room and a suicide in another. Those unhappy spirits were said to be trapped at the Driskill. But they were not alone.

This prestigious hotel seems to be the afterlife abode of several ghosts. One who resides on the fifth floor—an African-American night watchman with a pocket watch—was known in life to be a faithful employee of the Driskill. After working at the hotel for more than 20 years, the gentleman retired and then passed away. For decades following his death, hotel guests would inquire about the fellow with the pocket watch who was manning the desk on the fifth floor.

In 1998 the Driskill's banquet manager, Arthur Cicchese, related an incredible supernatural experience he had at the hotel early one morning as he prepared to open the restaurant.

"Outside the restaurant, there's a double set of elevators," Cicchese explained, "and there's this mirror that covers the whole area in front of the elevators." Cicchese was standing directly in front of that mirror between the elevators, adjusting his tie, at just before six o'clock one morning.

"Both elevators started to swoop down," he said. "I could hear laughter getting louder and louder." When the elevators stopped at his level, Cicchese expected to see a group of late-night revelers spill out into the hall. Instead, both elevator doors opened simultaneously, revealing that they were absolutely empty. What startled Cicchese at that point was that the sound of laughter had grown even louder.

"I'm still looking in the mirror," Cicchese explained. "I see nothing behind me. Laughter is now [that of] several people, very loud. I feel this cold breeze behind my neck; [it gave me] goose bumps all over. I turn around and as I turn around, I still see nothing. But the laughter got even louder, as the spirits seemed to say, 'Look, he turned around to find us!' " As Arthur Cicchese realized that he had just been the object of spectral ridicule, the sound of the phantom merrymakers trailed off in the direction of the hotel's lobby.

"Now it was a good experience," Cicchese later recalled. "I didn't feel spooked or scared. I felt like, well, these were definitely several spirits that had been partying all night, and here it was—five thirty, quarter to six in the morning—[and they still] sounded like they were inebriated." Although it was Cicchese's first personal experience with the Driskill's paranormal side, he added that there were "a million other ghost stories floating around the hotel."

One Driskill ghost has even managed to become somewhat famous, immortalized in the 1992 single "Ghost of a Texas Ladies' Man" by the band Concrete Blonde. The band's singer, Johnette Napolitano, wrote the song after having her own strange encounter while staying at the Driskill.

In the April/May 1992 issue of *Network*, Napolitano recounted her experience. "The TV would work, and then it wouldn't," she said. "My key fit in the lock, and then it didn't...I went to bed that night, turned the light off and closed my eyes, and the light went back on."

Napolitano explained that the light was so persistent in turning itself on that she eventually resorted to unplugging the lamp. The ghost, however, would not be that easily discouraged. As Napolitano lay there in the dark, she suddenly heard a creaking sound. "I opened my eyes and the light was on in the closet and the door was creaking open, just like someone was opening it slowly," she said.

The singer was frightened but didn't let her fear get the better of her. She spoke calmly to the ghost, saying,

"I know you're here and I know you won't hurt me," then somehow managed to go to sleep.

In the light of day, Napolitano may have wondered if her imagination had been playing a trick on her. She was assured otherwise when talking to a drummer who was traveling on the same tour. He told her stories about a phantom on the fifth floor of the hotel that was known for making amorous advances toward female guests. "It only goes for single women," Napolitano concluded.

As fascinating as the hotel's supernatural activity is, it's just as amazing that the Driskill Hotel and its resident spirits are still in Austin. By 1970, despite the building's designation as a State Historic Landmark and its inclusion in the National Register of Historic Places, the wrecking ball was a real threat. The fading grande dame was about to be torn down and replaced by a parking lot when fate, in the form of a citizens' group led by the Austin Heritage Society, intervened. The group raised enough money to stop the demolition and renovate the building. It reopened in 1973, in true Driskill fashion, with a gala ball.

Since then, the hotel has gone through several periods of extensive refurbishing and renovation. That care and attention has made the Driskill once again the magnificent and historic heart of the capital. Now in its second century, it manages to graciously showcase its past while offering every possible comfort and convenience of the modern age.

If, on occasion, that past intrudes a bit on the present-day landscape with a sudden chill or a shifting shadow that suggests an unexpected visitor from days gone by, most people are understanding and even welcoming. After all, over the decades the Driskill set the scene for countless dramas and even starred in a few. It is understandable that some ghosts have chosen to return to such an emotionally and energetically charged location.

Arthur Cicchese summed it up well in 1998 when he said, "The building is 112 years old, you should expect that there are some spirits floating around," then added his personal assessment, "I think they're all friendly."

A glorious Texas hotel, populated by agreeable ghosts: that's the Driskill, embodying the true "spirit" of southern hospitality.

Myrtles Plantation

If you ever pay a visit to the grand antebellum mansion known as Myrtles Plantation and a man in khaki pants meets you at the front gate and tells you that the property is closed, don't believe him. He is only one of the many ghosts who haunt the Louisiana plantation—one who, obviously, would prefer not to have quite so much company.

That particular apparition is unlikely to get his wish. This incredible historic mansion is now a thriving bed and breakfast, despite the fact—or perhaps because of the fact—that it is tremendously ghost-ridden. If you'd like a second opinion, check with the Smithsonian Institute, which has seen fit to include Myrtles Plantation on its list of the most haunted places in the world.

The owners of the plantation will be happy to confirm this. They have never tried to avoid the supernatural subject. Quite the contrary—and possibly because it was pointless to do otherwise—they appear to embrace it.

"Mystery tours" on Friday and Saturday evenings feature chillingly detailed stories about their resident specters. Visitors can purchase "good luck voodoo dolls" in the gift shop. And those who shop for edible delights in the "Butler's Pantry" are kept honest by a sign that reminds them "God and our ghost are watching you."

That should be *ghosts*—plural. Myrtles Plantation is home to a great many spirits, probably because it was built over a desecrated American Indian burial ground and has had a notably bloody past. The plantation has been the site of at least 10 murders, and several of the ghosts are directly linked to those horrifying, historic events.

A prominent lawyer named William Winter was one of the people who met a violent end at Myrtles Plantation. He bought the mansion in 1861 and was murdered there 10 years later, when a man who called Winter out on the veranda shot him squarely in the chest. Winter didn't expire immediately. Clutching his blood-soaked chest, he was able to stagger back into the elegant foyer and up 17 steps of the main staircase. There, he collapsed and died in front of his horrified wife, who had heard the shot and had come running to the second-floor landing. To this day, Winter's spirit seems to be trapped in the moment of his murder. People frequently hear his ghost thumping across the entrance way and up exactly 17 of the 20 stairs.

Years before Winter was killed, another violent drama played out at Myrtles Plantation. It started when the daughter of the house, a child named Sarah, contracted yellow fever. When the finest doctors were unable to heal her, Sarah's father sent for a powerful voodoo priestess who was a slave at a neighboring plantation. When the slave, Clio, arrived, she was told that she would either save the child's life—or lose her own. Despite this "motivation," Sarah's fever had progressed to a point where even Clio's magic could not save her. She died in her bed. The girl's father, mad with grief, hanged Clio from the chandelier in his daughter's bedroom. Today, guests can sleep in the antique four-poster where Sarah succumbed to her illness. Fair warning is given, however—they may awaken to see Clio shaking her magic gris-gris bag over the bed or to hear her low, mumbling incantations as she tries to save both Sarah and herself.

The most famous murders at Myrtles Plantation involved another owner, Judge Clarke Woodruffe, and a slave named Chloe. Chloe had the enviable assignment of caring for the judge's children inside the comfortable mansion. She was also his mistress. When Woodruffe turned his wandering attentions to another slave, Chloe became jealous. Perhaps because she wondered if her luxurious days of indoor labor were numbered, she began eavesdropping on the master's conversations. She was unfortunate enough to be caught listening to Woodruffe as he planned some less-than-legal business scheme and was summarily punished. Judge Woodruffe had Chloe's left ear sliced off to provide her with a permanent reminder of her misdeed.

Soon after, wearing a green turban to hide her disfigurement, Chloe made a meek gesture of reconciliation. She offered to bake a special cake for the birthday of one of the children. The judge accepted and Chloe set to work, using a recipe known only to her. The recipe included mashed oleander leaves—a lethal poison.

There are those who say that Chloe intended only to make the family sick so that she might nurse them back to health, thereby reinstating herself in the judge's good books. There are others who insist that what she did was nothing more or less than brutal revenge. But no matter what her original intentions were, there was a deadly amount of oleander lacing the cake. Judge Woodruffe was called away on business and missed the celebration, but his wife and two daughters ate generous slices of the poisoned confection and died horrible, lingering deaths.

Little time was wasted. Chloe was hanged from one of the plantation's massive oak trees and her body was thrown into the river. Her spirit has never left Myrtles Plantation—nor have the spirits of the two blonde children who died of the slave's "sweet revenge." The little girls, in their long, white dresses, have often been seen playing on the mansion's expansive veranda. On other occasions, guests have been startled to see the girls' pale, little faces staring at them—from outside the second-floor windows. Chloe, recognizable in her green turban, wanders throughout the house and grounds. She is the ghost most often encountered at the plantation and has even been captured on film. Should you spend a night there, don't be alarmed if you awaken to see her leaning anxiously over your bed, peering down at you. Chloe, in her ethereal form, is really quite harmless. She may even tuck you in—she's done it before.

There are many other ghosts at the plantation who simply seem to be trapped in their earthly routines. There is a phantom child who likes to jump on the bed of one first-floor suite and the spectral maid who follows behind her, smoothing the bed covers. The grand piano has been known to play by itself, but only when no one is standing near it. The apparition of a woman in a long, black dress swirls to unheard music in one particular bedroom. There is no mistaking her for a living person, for her waltzing feet float at least 10 inches above the floor. Also, according to Dennis William Hauck's *Haunted Places: The National Directory* (Penguin Books, 1996), "Ghosts from the slave graveyard on the property [have been known to] report for chores..." All in all, 14 distinct spirits are believed to haunt the plantation house. It is impossible to know how many are wandering the grounds.

So if the real-looking entity at the gate tries to steer you away, don't allow him to succeed. If he does, you'll be missing a marvelous experience: a night within the confines of an authentic mansion, steeped in history, charm and authentic antebellum ghosts.

CHAPTER V

Britain's Ghostly Guests

Molesworth Arms Hotel

"Aunt Rose always says you've got far more to fear from the living than the dead."

Those were words that Sarah Dibb found comforting after she discovered that the 16th-century coaching inn that she managed in Wadebridge, Cornwall, truly was haunted. There had long been stories associated with the historic hotel, but Dibb had originally believed them to be no more than colorful legends. Locals spoke of a murdered chambermaid whose spirit roamed through the guest rooms, the phantom of an odd, little man who played mischievous tricks and a headless coachman who would drive his coach and horses through the hotel's archway at exactly midnight on New Year's Eve.

A headless coachman?

"I still think that's just a myth," said Dibb in 1998. But by that time, she had come to accept that the two other ghosts were quite real.

At first the clues were subtle.

"I'd come in in the morning and unlock. And often I felt that there was someone in the kitchen with me. I'd always seem to see this little old man out of the corner of my eye. I would think he was there, but then when I'd look properly, he was not."

Dibb might have dismissed the strange sensation had it not been accompanied by a number of other mysteries. The cups, which were always set out upside down on the saucers, were often turned right side up, and the spoons would be set in them. Bottles would occasionally "jump" off the shelves as well—a ghostly phenomenon that was difficult to ignore. In room 20, the kettle would frequently switch on and off by itself. Then, finally, there came the day when any lingering doubts that Sarah Dibb might have had were completely banished. Dibb's mother, who occasionally worked in the Molesworth Arms kitchen, actually *saw* one of the spirits.

"He was a wizened, little, old man, wearing a black coat. He had gray hair in a pony tail. He just walked right through the kitchen! My mother saw him—nobody else did," noted Sarah.

It was then that Sarah Dibb and her mother decided to place a telephone call to "Aunt Rose," an old family friend in Brighton, who had a measure of psychic talent.

"We laughingly call her a 'witch,' my mother and I," explained Dibb. "She has visions and things. Not regularly—sometimes it's very strong with her, and other times it's not. It comes and it goes."

Fortunately for Dibb, Aunt Rose was decidedly "on" when she attempted to psychically tune in to the spectral happenings at the hotel. She immediately informed Dibb that the spirit of the old man was named "Charlie" and that he had once been a sort of caretaker who had done odd jobs around the Molesworth Arms in return for food and lodging.

"She described Charlie to a 'T,' as my mum had seen him. She described the top floor of the hotel exactly—having never been here. She said that the hotel was definitely haunted by Charlie—and she said that there was one other."

Dibb believed the other spirit to be the murdered chambermaid.

"We actually think she's the one in room 20, which is the really haunted room where the kettle likes to switch itself on and off." Noting that there was supernatural activity in room 3 as well, Dibb explained, "The actual story of it goes that she was murdered in room 3 and then her body was dragged up to the top floor, where room 20 is. I think it was around the 1700s, quite early in the history of the building, really."

Though the haunting seems to be primarily directed at the staff, Dibb confessed that guests would occasionally notice the ghostly goings-on.

"We had one guest that stayed in room 3," she recalled, "and she said, 'Oh, have you got a ghost?' We said, 'Yes,' and she said, 'Oh, thank goodness for that! I thought I was going mad!' "

Generally, tourists love the town of Wadebridge for its tranquillity, its history and its location on North Cornwall's Heritage Coastline. But for those who seek a mysterious thrill mixed in with their Cornish hospitality, there will always be "Charlie" and the Molesworth Arms Hotel.

The Mermaid Inn

Rye, in East Sussex, is sometimes said to be the most beautiful town in Britain. Any person who has enjoyed its picturesque charm can understand why. Sloping cobblestone streets, 16th-century timbered houses and breathtaking views of the lush countryside all combine to create an archetypal English village. As a result, Rye has a thriving tourist trade woven of quaint tea shops, antiques, museums and the town's dramatic history.

Rye flourished as a port town before the harbor choked with silt and the sea retreated. It followed that smugglers and pirates played a huge part in the area's history and its fortunes. It is a matter of fact that by the 18th century, Rye's prosperity depended as much upon smuggling as it did upon any legitimate trade. When English evangelist John Wesley visited the town in 1773, he found the people "willing to hear the good word," but "unwilling to part with the accursed smuggling."

And so the smugglers thrived and shaped the history of the town—including the history of one of its oldest hostelries, the Mermaid Inn.

The Mermaid Inn, as it stands today, dates back to the early 15th century. Its cellar and foundations, though, are thought to be from as early as 1150. During the time when Rye thrived on illegal trade, the inn was a notorious smuggler's haunt. Today, many believe it is haunted by smugglers…

Those infamous days are evident in certain secret elements of the building's architecture. The Mermaid Inn has hidden staircases, rooms with moving wall panels and a concealed entrance to a "priest's hole" through the back of the cupboard above the bar fireplace. Rye's smugglers left behind more than a few secret passageways, however. They also left ghosts, making the Mermaid Inn one of historic Rye's most haunted places.

Guests in room 5 at the inn, known as the "Nutcracker Suite," have frequently been visited by the "Lady in White." She drifts across the rooms and through the closed door, pausing briefly, only once, at the foot of the bed. She is believed to have been a girl who worked at the Mermaid Inn in the 1700s. She fell in love with a smuggler, they say and was murdered for being too indiscreet about her man's criminal activities. Today, as she wanders through the inn, she is believed to be searching for her ruthless lover.

The Elizabethan Chamber, room 16, is the scene of one of the inn's most incredible spectral shows. One night during the 1930s, a guest who was staying in the room awakened to see that a spectacular, silent duel was taking place in her midst. The combatants were dressed in Renaissance-era costumes and were battling with rapiers. The fight raged on until at last, one of the men was run through with a blade. The victor then dragged his opponent's bleeding body to the corner of the room, pulled open a secret trap door and threw the corpse down the passageway.

According to the inn's staff, "The body thrown down the stairs of the secret passage would have landed in the bar section. The barman, a few years ago, was tending to his fire when all the bottles on the shelf at the other end of the room fell [to the floor]. He handed his notice in the next day."

Few could blame the man for not wanting to work in a

bar where invisible corpses could come flying into the room at any time, creating a great mess.

A number of other phantoms at the Mermaid Inn are not as obviously associated with any particular era. In room 1, known as "Cadmans," many guests have reported seeing a lady wearing either white or gray, sitting in the chair by the fireplace. Others, who have not necessarily seen the ghost, have complained that they draped their clothing over the chair at night and found it in the morning to be soaking wet. The staff maintains that "there are no windows or pipe works anywhere near the chair."

Of course, comfortable chairs—particularly rocking chairs—rarely remain unoccupied at the Mermaid Inn. A chambermaid once frantically told her supervisor, "A rocking chair is moving on its own—quite fast, too—and I didn't touch it!" When the supervisor first went into the room to investigate, the chair was sitting still. But before she could leave the room, it began to rock again. As the supervisor stared in amazement, she noticed that the cushion on the chair had compressed as though a heavy person was sitting on it.

Although the rocking chair specter was invisible, most of the ghosts at the inn seem quite willing to show their faces. Quite a number of apparitions—usually dressed in old-fashioned garments—have been seen in the rooms. Sometimes they walk the corridors too, as a chambermaid named Kate Davis learned.

Davis was walking down one of the halls one morning when she noticed a woman approaching from the opposite direction. As the two passed each another, Davis offered a cheery "Good morning!" She received no reply. Davis must have been taken aback by the guest's rudeness and turned around to look at her. All Davis saw, however, was a long, empty hallway and no door through which the woman could have vanished.

Judith Blincow, who purchased the Mermaid Inn in 1993 and has worked there since the mid-1980s, once said, "Although I have not personally seen ghosts, I certainly have met some very convinced and frightened guests."

They were guests who had no doubt witnessed more than their share of "the living history" in the enchanting and popular town of Rye.

The Talbot

The first thing mentioned in brochures from the Talbot Hotel in Oundle, Northamptonshire, is its ghost. This is understandable, given that she is a spirit of impressive pedigree—none other than Mary, Queen of Scots.

"It is hardly surprising that the ghost of Mary, Queen of Scots should haunt the Talbot Hotel..." the brochures say. Not that the tragic queen ever set foot in the structure, parts of which date back to A.D. 638. Rather, Mary's ethereal form is believed to have traveled there—along with stones, beams of wood and other building materials scavenged from the nearby ruins of Fotheringhay Castle, where she was imprisoned prior to her execution.

In 1626 the frontage of the Talbot was rebuilt, using stones taken from the castle. Twelve years later, the proprietor installed Fotheringhay's oak staircase in his hotel, along with the great windows that sit above the stairwell. It was the very staircase that the doomed queen descended on the last morning of her life. The windows were the ones through which she watched the preparations for her execution. And, if that was not enough to draw Mary's forlorn spirit to the hotel, the Talbot was where her executioner stayed on the night before he beheaded her.

It is said that since those 17th-century renovations, the queen wanders through two of the Talbot's suites and drifts sadly up and down the famous staircase. Sometimes she is heard sobbing—it is a ghostly sound that can continue for hours and is impossible to follow to its source. Sometimes she is seen—guests have reported a mournful-looking woman in a long, black dress, standing at the foot of their bed or gazing sadly through the windows by the stairs. Also, there is a mark on the polished wooden balustrade in the shape of a crown. It is said to have been made by the ring on Mary's hand as she gripped that railing on her way to the block. Centuries of buffing have not managed to diminish the eerie scar.

Though the story sounds like a legend, one former employee insists that it is not.

"We had several people who saw the ghost of Mary, Queen of Scots, including myself," the woman insisted.

And, as for the ring mark?

"That is still there and was verified by experts from London many years ago as being genuine," she said.

Oundle's historians say that up until the last couple of centuries, there was one other paranormal reason to visit the Talbot: an old right-of-way at the back of the hotel known as "Drumming Well Lane."

It became known as such in the middle of the 17th century, when it was discovered that a well on the street emitted a loud drumming sound prophesying national disasters. The well became quite famous, according to one traveler of the day, quoted in Talbot Hotel literature:

> There is much discourse of a strange well at Oundle…wherein a kind of drumming in manner of a march has been heard; it is said to be very ominous, having been heard heretofore and always precedes some great accident. I wrote to the town for an account of it and was informed of the truth of it, and that it beat for a fortnight the latter end of last month and the beginning of this and was heard in the very same manner before the late King's death, the death of [Oliver] Cromwell, the King's coming in and the Fire of London.

Eventually the well ceased to drum. Then came the day when it was filled in. Today, only the street name remains to remind people of the ghostly sound that once predicted some of England's greatest tragedies.

Dalhousie Castle

Although only a 20-minute drive from Edinburgh, Dalhousie Castle is world away from the Scottish capital. As it sits alongside the River South Esk, in the rolling Midlothian countryside, it is a vision of splendor and a reminder of Scotland's turbulent past.

It was built in the 13th century by the Ramsays of Dalhousie, a noble Scottish family. That the castle was once a defensive fortress is still evident in the architecture, particularly near the main entrance. There, one can see the original recesses for the counterbalance beams of the drawbridge-raising mechanism, as well as narrow openings in the parapets through which the castle's defenders could drop missiles or pour boiling oil.

Today, quite to the contrary, everyone who visits the castle is met with warm Scottish hospitality. Guests can enjoy beautifully styled en suite bedrooms, fine dining and a host of leisure pursuits. Those who prefer to relax indoors can do so in the comfort of the library, surrounded by an extensive collection of fine books and nestled in front of a crackling fire. Should a guest catch a staff member in a storytelling mood, he might even hear about Dalhousie's very own ghosts...

It is said that there are several.

An employee named Jackie recalled one particular incident involving an American woman who arrived at Dalhousie Castle in the early 1990s. Jackie showed the woman to the reception area and waited as the receptionist began registering her as a guest.

"About half way through booking in," Jackie recalled, "she suddenly threw her key back and asked [me] to get

Dalhousie Castle near Edinburgh, Scotland

her a taxi. The receptionist and myself asked what was the matter, and she said, 'There are too many spirits in this place and I won't be able to relax!' [Then] off she went, leaving us speechless!"

Despite being rendered "speechless," Jackie couldn't have been entirely surprised. She had once had her hair tugged by a playful specter and was present when an elderly guest was touched by a ghost during a wedding reception.

"Another staff member…and myself were alone in the [Brechin] room with the elderly gentleman, who was smoking a cigar and talking to us. Suddenly the gentleman stopped talking and started looking over both his shoulders. The color drained from his face and he looked as if he was going to faint. We got him a chair and a glass of water."

Once the man had calmed down, he told Jackie and her co-worker what had happened.

"He said someone kept tapping him on the shoulders,

[moving] from one to the other—but we knew that there was no one else there!"

"I've heard many strange tales," Jackie admitted, "from past staff members and from guests."

It is interesting to note that not all of those phantoms have originated from the castle's early years. Many are the result of recent history. According to Dalhousie Castle documents, the structure served as a primary public school from approximately 1925 to 1950. During that time, records show that a schoolboy jumped to his death from the top of the castle. Ever since the tragic event, there have been reports of the boy's spirit returning. During the Christmas of 1996, the five-year-old son of guests insisted that he had a "friend" who stayed with him in his room. The boy's playmate was distinguishable in that he was ever so invisible.

Another haunting in recent years involves a phantom of the four-legged variety. "Petra" the dog died in the 1980s when it was startled into jumping from the top tower of the castle. Since then, the little dog has been scurrying up the stairs and along the castle corridors.

"I can only assume [that it's] looking for its master!" said Andrew Sharp, the castle steward and pipe sergeant. Sharp has seen the spectral dog on several occasions. He's also seen the entity known as "Lady Catherine," who is believed to date back to approximately 1720.

"[She's also] known as the 'Gray Lady,'" Sharp explained, "because of her dress...She travels the stairs, the dungeon and the 'Black' corridor, originally the lower battlements. It appears that she does not like bagpipe music because when [she's] seen by me, the bagpipes failed to play in a sweet tune.

"I met her on three occasions when playing," Sharp said. "She died of a broken heart and the want of food, or so it is said."

It is almost surprising that there aren't more ghosts haunting Dalhousie Castle, given its occasionally violent history. One of the enduring reminders of those times is the forbidding "Bottle Dungeon." Prisoners had to be lowered into the tiny, windowless prison by ropes. The stonework still shows the score marks made by those who were held captive there.

But that was then. Today, guests find the perfect combination of world-class hospitality, fascinating history and authentic phantoms at the magnificent Dalhousie Castle.

Lord Crewe Arms Hotel

The village of Blanchland in northern England's County Durham is pretty and remote, tucked in the heather-covered hills of the northern Pennines. There, you'll find the Lord Crewe Arms Hotel. The 12th-century hewn-stone structure is home to what Robert P. Long, author of *Castle Hotels of Europe* (Prentice-Hall International, 1982), calls "one of Britain's most authenticated ghosts."

Lord Crewe Arms appears to house several ghosts, actually—many of them monks from the days when the hotel was not a hotel but "Blanchland Abbey." The White Canons built the monastery in 1165 and occupied it for nearly 400 years.

"Theirs are the footsteps worn into the stone," wrote Alen MacWeeney in the October 1996 issue of *Travel*

Holiday. "You can still feel the spirits of the old monks here, ingrained in the stone walls that were quarried during the Crusades."

According to some of the hotel's guests, you can more than "feel" the spirits. You can see and touch them. Members of the staff recalled one particularly memorable incident from the mid-1990s:

> ...[A] couple were sleeping in the Radcliffe bedroom. They did not know that the room that they were in was part of the abbot's lodging of a...monastery and they knew nothing of the White Canons. The wife woke during the night to see a monk in a white habit kneeling at the bottom of her four-poster bed. She put her hand out [to touch him and found that] he was quite solid. Then, she reported, he slowly dematerialized. Her husband was asleep beside her and we know that they had drunk very little at dinner the previous evening.

One has to presume that the ghost of any monk who haunts the Lord Crewe Arms has been doing so for nearly 500 years, for the abbey was dissolved early in the 16th century. The abbey itself eventually fell into ruin, but the abbot's lodging, guest house and kitchen evolved into a manor house inhabited by several subsequent owners. In 1701, the estate was inherited by Tom Forster and his sister, Dorothy.

Tom Forster was the commander of the Jacobite forces during the uprising of 1715. He was eventually captured by the government army and imprisoned. Three days before he was to stand trial for treason, his sister Dorothy helped him to escape. She spirited her brother back to the Lord Crewe Arms and hid him away in the "priest's hole," which still exists today, high inside the chimney of the home's massive stone fireplace. Tom Forster was eventually able to make his way to France, where he spent the remainder of his days.

Dorothy, it is believed, is now spending eternity in her former home. It is she who is considered "one of Britain's most authenticated ghosts." According to those at the Lord Crewe Arms, her spirit haunts the Bamburgh Room, a charming guest room with mullioned windows overlooking the walled gardens. She has appeared to numerous people, pleading with anyone who will listen to take a message to her brother.

"All is well now," Dorothy's ghost says. "Tom can safely return to England."

But, to date, Tom Forster's spirit has not been seen. He must be either resting peacefully or spending the afterlife exiled in France, unaware that times have changed.

This excerpt of a verse is taken from a brochure for the hotel:

Precious gem of a village, set with hills all around
Where history and mystery and legends abound.

It is poetry that neatly summarizes the appeal of both Blanchland and the Lord Crewe Arms Hotel.

Comlongon Castle

Comlongon Castle is a 14th-century fortress and mansion set on 120 acres of secluded grounds near the town of Dumfries. In recent years, the medieval keep, with its refurbished great hall, has become one of the most popular wedding venues in Scotland.

"We're getting quite a reputation now for organizing weddings," said Phillip Ptolemy, a member of the family that owns the castle. "We do about 200 a year now."

Ptolemy sees a certain irony in that fact—considering that one of the most notorious events in the castle's history involved a wedding engagement that ended in tragedy.

Back in the year 1570, Sir James Douglas obtained permission to marry a young woman named Lady Marion Carruthers. Douglas was not in love with Marion so much as he had designs on her estate, a fact of which the lady was quite aware. The unhappy bride-to-be tried every means of dissuading Douglas. None worked. She then tried to escape, seeking sanctuary in Comlongon Castle, which was her uncle's home. But Sir James Douglas refused to give up. He sued through the courts for what he called his "just inheritance." It was determined that Douglas had a valid marriage contract. Lady Marion was ordered by the courts to surrender herself to her betrothed. Instead, she chose to throw herself from the battlements of Comlongon Castle, thereby resolving the matter once and for all.

Or did she?

There were those who suspected that Douglas' men forced their way into Lady Marion's chamber and threw her to her death, so that Sir James might claim the estate without having the bother of such a willful wife. But, officially, Marion's death was ruled a suicide. On September 25, 1570, it was recorded that Lady Marion Carruthers "did willfully take her own life by leaping from the lookout tower of Comlongon Castle and did break her head and bones." Because she was believed to have died by her own hand, Marion was denied a proper Christian burial. Ever since, her restless spirit has remained trapped within the castle walls.

"There are some people who have actually seen her," said Phillip Ptolemy. "But more often it's things like the bedclothes getting ripped off the beds, personal items going missing and turning up in very strange locations or paperwork [being] sorted.

"Very strange things," he admitted.

And it is not only members of the Ptolemy family who have experienced the ghostly lady. Guests have been known to meet her as well.

"We get stories from people who aren't aware of the situation at all," Ptolemy said. "They'll say, 'Is there a ghost here?' And we have to say, 'Well, yes, there is.' There's certainly something here. It's hard to pin it down, but there's definitely something."

One of the reasons Ptolemy has found it difficult to "pin [the haunting] down" is Lady Marion's subtle ghostly approach. At times it can be frustrating.

"The majority of the experiences border on explainable," said Ptolemy. "There's just that element of doubt all the time. If it was just one or two isolated stories, you could dismiss them. But when they regularly happen, on a weekly basis, there's a pattern."

Beyond this pattern of minor incidents, there have

been occasions when Lady Marion has seen fit to make her presence undeniably known. Phillip Ptolemy recalled one such event:

"My brother was thrown across the room by her," he said. "There were several of us there when it happened. It was in a room where we have a bar, and he was just leaning against the bar, and the next thing was that he was just thrown across the room. He was just as white as a sheet afterward."

And then there is the other bit of eerie proof that Lady Marion does not rest easily. From the time of her death, it was noticed that no grass would grow on the piece of ground where she fell. More than 400 years later, this is still the case.

"Grass still doesn't grow there," Phillip Ptolemy confirmed. "It's a very dead area..."

...And Comlongon would appear to be a very haunted castle, well worth a visit for any fan of the paranormal.

Dryburgh Abbey Hotel

In the breathtaking Scottish Borders countryside on the banks of the River Tweed sit the ruins of Dryburgh Abbey. What remains here, in this place where Sir Walter Scott was laid to rest, has been called the most beautiful and remarkably complete of all the Border Abbeys. Situated beside it in a magnificent manor house is the equally impressive Dryburgh Abbey Hotel.

Though the house dates back to only 1845, there had been another house on the site for many years before. A dramatic story, involving a resident of the original house, has been passed down through the generations.

It is said that in the time when the abbey was still in use, one of the resident monks entered into a love affair with the young lady of the house. The abbot, upon hearing of this infidelity, ordered that the monk be put to death. His orders were carried out immediately. The young lady was so distraught over the loss of her lover that she threw herself into the Tweed and drowned. The lasting result of that tragedy has been the ghost—generally known as the "Gray Lady"—who now haunts the hotel and grounds.

"We had quite a few sightings of the Gray Lady, especially in one of the bedrooms," said John Sloggie, who managed the hotel from 1991 through 1997. "[Guests had seen] images of her by the window and by the door. She was also seen in the out buildings, on the hotel grounds and on the chain bridge which goes out over the river..."

According to the current manager, Fiona Fleming, little changed after Sloggie's time at Dryburgh Abbey Hotel. Fleming herself has encountered the spirit, although she

Dryburgh Abbey Hotel, home to the "Gray Lady"

has never caught sight of her famous misty-gray form.

"You tend to feel her more than actually see her," Fleming explained. "You can go into the bar and the radiators are roasting hot, but the bar's freezing cold."

According to staff, the Gray Lady tends to make herself known especially when changes are taking place within the hotel. During the winter of 1992, the hotel closed and underwent an ambitious renovation. During that time, there were often as many as 65 tradesmen on site, handling various elements of construction. It was reported that many mysterious "happenings" took place then. More recently, during periods of comparatively minor upheaval, the ghost still appears to resist change.

"It still tends to happen if we're doing building work within the hotel," said Fleming. "If we're sort of changing anything, there tends to be more activity then."

But the conservative manager hesitated to be too specific about the exact kind of activity. Though the Gray Lady is mentioned in hotel literature, Fiona Fleming tended to remain low-key about her, acknowledging that the paranormal is not every guest's cup of tea.

"We are careful who we mention the ghost to," she said. "Americans coming over love it, though. It's the old country house with the ghost, you know."

She claimed that locals took a more prosaic view of such things.

"In this country, it's not a big deal really, I don't suppose."

Of course not. Just a typical "Gray Lady" ghost in another run-of-the-mill mansion near some everyday historical ruins set in the average majesty of the Scottish countryside. That is the Dryburgh Abbey Hotel, and all it has to offer.

Finnygook Inn/Sconner House Inn

The Finnygook is a 16th-century inn situated in Crafthole, between the sea and the green Cornish countryside. They tell a story there that begins, "Once upon a time in the 18th century a notorious smuggler called Silas Finny lived locally…"

Finny was less famous for his crimes than he was for his betrayal of several fellow law breakers. It was believed that there was a disagreement among them, following which Finny tipped off the excise men regarding the details of an expected shipment of cargo. The tip resulted in the arrests of several of the smugglers. They were deported to Botany Bay in Australia under the watch of Captain Bligh. According to the account, "They did not have an enjoyable time."

Finny was doomed in his own way. It is said that he was "foully done to death at Bligers Well…no doubt as a lesson to fellow renegades." But Finny refused to accept his lesson in a good-natured fashion. His ghost is said to remain in the area, haunting the locals. Some, they say, "will not walk between Crafthole and Portwrinkle during the dark hours…"

• • •

"I don't know if you're aware, but the name 'Finnygook' is Cornish for 'Finny's Ghost.' [Also,] from underneath the car park of the Finnygook Inn, there is a tunnel that goes down the hill, underneath the cliffs to the beach, which was used by the smugglers of old."

These were tidbits of information from one who would know—a fellow named Clifford Porter, who once ran the bar at the Finnygook Inn. In a letter dated August 14, 1997, Porter explained that he knew that the smuggler's ghost existed, for he had once seen him "sitting in the restaurant, smoking a long, clay pipe and in the sea-going dress of his day." The former barman also lamented that he "suffered a fair bit" at Finny's phantom hands while employed at the inn.

Porter claimed that the spirit was often the most active in the beer cellar. He was once plagued by a banging noise there that was so loud and insistent, he was forced to leave the cellar.

"This occurred several times," Porter recalled, "and when once I turned around and shouted, 'Go away and leave me alone!' a spanner [wrench] came flying through the air and dented the wall next to me head, showering me with pieces of brick. Needless to say, I did not hang around and I never shouted again!"

But as the barman, Porter couldn't avoid the beer cellar. Whenever a keg ran dry, he had to go into the little room to change over the lines. He said, "It was nothing to discover that a line had already been disconnected in readiness for the changeover." This, despite the unsettling fact that Porter was the only person who possessed a key to the room. Finny's ghost was also fond of turning off the gas taps in the locked cellar, causing all of the beer lines to run dry.

On one March day in 1992, a group of school children visited the Finnygook Inn with their teacher. The purpose of the field trip was to learn about Silas Finny. Clifford Porter was regaling the students with stories when they asked if they might see the cellar for themselves.

"We had been there three or four minutes," Porter wrote, "when one child suddenly shouted, 'Come on out Captain Finny, wherever you are!' [At the time], three barrels of beer exploded, one by one, and soaked us all!"

Porter, noting that he was the one who had to mop up, complained, "He is a very bad-tempered ghost."

Clifford Porter is qualified to make such a judgment, having witnessed a number of spirits in his day. When he left the Finnygook Inn, it was to become manager of the Sconner House Inn, owned by the same family, in the neighboring village of Polbathic. There, he found other specters awaiting him.

At Sconner House, Porter wrote, guests would sometimes request a change of room, "owing to a small curly-headed boy of about five or six years of age, dressed all in blue and with knickers as trousers." The child would come out of the en suite, walk across the bedroom floor and glide straight out onto the grounds through the closed window.

"He's only seen on dull or rainy days," wrote Porter, "and only about four or five times a year.

"One of our guests was very shaken up when he tried to talk with him in the bushes of the gardens, only to watch the boy fade away."

The other apparition at the Sconner House Inn is a lady in a long, black dress.

"She either 'hovers' upon our staircase or floats across the bottom of our driveway towards the river on the other side of the road," explained Porter. Several guests have reported seeing her over the years. According to some, she can be mistaken for a flesh-and-blood person. Clifford Porter recalled "one old lady [who] burst out laughing to several people in the bar and proclaimed to all that she had been trying to talk to a dead person! The bar emptied out soon after that," he recalled, "which reinforces my notion that ghosts are really very bad for business."

Unfortunately for Clifford Porter, he seems destined to deal with such paranormal creatures during both his business and leisure hours. Though the following story took place in Porter's personal life and not in either of the inns, it is too irresistible not to include here.

"In my tender years," he wrote, "I used to 'talk' with a black dog. This is my mother's story, for I cannot recall this. My mother thought that this was the usual childhood 'make-believe' friend [for several months]. Then one day, she saw it for herself. She flooded the house with clergymen and priests and the dog was seen no more.

"[Then,] after my wife and I got married...we moved into an old terraced house in Eastbourne, East Sussex. I kept seeing a black dog that seemed to be waiting for me when I came home from the office! I ransacked the house, totally, many a time, searching for this dog, but I could never find where it went.

"One night, when we had some friends around to the house for drinks, a 'scratching' was heard in the hallway. One of our friends opened the door and called out, 'It's a dog!' I shouted to him to catch it. He bent down, [reached for the dog,] and his hands and arms went straight through it! The dog then vanished; he and his wife passed out, as did two others; you can imagine the chaos! It was difficult hosting parties after that..."

Porter wrote that he and his wife had never told the story of the black dog to their son—and so had been quite shocked by a comment made by his young granddaughter, Alice, during a visit in early August 1997.

"She suddenly turned to my wife," wrote Porter, "after I had left the room and asked, 'Why does Grandad always have a black dog with him?' When questioned by my upset wife, Alice said that every time she comes here, she sees this dog following along behind me. This has unsettled me well, as you can imagine."

On the general subject of ghosts, Clifford Porter concluded, "While they are interesting, I for one can do without them!"

Unfortunately for this haunted, personable innkeeper, the spirits seem both unlikely and unwilling to leave him alone.

Weston Manor Hotel

Weston Manor—which was first a monastery, then a manor house and since 1983 a hotel—has a history that dates back to the 11th century. During that time, the building was always considered to be the showpiece of its lovely Oxfordshire village, Weston-on-the-Green. That remains true today, as the imposing stone mansion offers its guests a peaceful retreat in elegant surroundings.

The 37 bedrooms all have garden views and private baths. Though it is not mentioned in the hotel's brochure, one also comes with a complimentary ghost—a young female presence who is affectionately known as "Mad Maude."

Maude, it is said, was a nun from a nearby convent back in the time when Weston Manor was a monastery. The nuns would come to the monastery for religious devotions—but Maude was unfortunate enough to develop a devotion of a more common sort. She fell passionately in love with one of the young monks and they began to meet in secret.

One night, the lovers were discovered in the monk's cell. Maude was found guilty of breaking her chastity vow and of causing another to do the same. There is nothing to indicate that her lover was punished for his part of the crime, so perhaps Maude paid for them both. She was chained to a stake and bundles of dry twigs were stacked around her feet. A torch was touched to the kindling and Maude was burned alive.

But it did not serve to banish the girl from the premises. Her spirit returned to haunt the scene of her passion and torturous execution, and it remains there to this very day.

Many guests who have stayed in Weston Manor's exquisite oak-paneled bedroom have reported the presence of something "malevolent." Perhaps Mad Maude requires a bit more time to get over the unfair treatment that she received at the hands of the monks...

At least two other, less famous spirits have been reported at the hotel. One is a cavalier, who has been seen sitting in the entrance hall sipping wine. The other is a phantom coach that roars through the otherwise tranquil garden at the rear of the house. There was once an elderly gardener who had seen the coach so many times, he refused to cross its customary path. To avoid a possible collision with the apparition, which would appear without notice, the gentleman always walked the long way around the yard.

It was once noted that "it would be strange if so ancient a house did not have some ghost stories associated with its previous inhabitants." Fortunately, Weston Manor Hotel has a good many spirits to show for its long and varied history.

The Bell

In 1802 the town of Thetford, in Norfolk, was a busy stop on the main thoroughfare between London and Norwich. Endless cargoes of goods were transported along this route, while businessmen and aristocrats traveled through the town. Anyone who stopped over looking for a meal or a bed likely stopped at the Bell Hotel.

The Bell, which had been around since the 15th century, was owned and operated in those days by a woman named Betty Radcliffe. The few stories that exist about Betty suggest that she was no shrinking violet. Being a businesswoman in her time would have required a degree of gritty determination, a quality that no doubt spilled over into her private life. When Betty saw something she wanted, she had it. When she wanted one of the ostlers who worked in the hotel's stables, she initiated a passionate love affair with him.

Betty was known to entertain her lover in what is now room 10 of the hotel. On their last evening together there, the two engaged in a bitter quarrel. It is said that she had tired of the man and ended the affair and that he was unhappy about being so easily dismissed. On that night, the relationship came to an ugly and violent end as the enraged ostler murdered Betty Radcliffe. When the landlady's last breath left her body, her staring eyes likely would have been focused upon the large, colorful, Elizabethan wall mural that dominated the room.

It's been 200 years since then, and much has changed in Thetford. The town is quieter, more reserved; it is now known more for the massive, unspoiled forests that surround it than it is for its bustling trade. The Bell Hotel has

The ghost of murdered innkeeper Betty Radcliffe haunts room 10 of the Bell in Thetford, Norfolk.

changed as well. It has gone through significant renovations and has been modernized to offer guests every convenience and creature comfort.

The wall mural, however, remains in room 10. It has faded with time and has been covered over with large, protective panes of glass, but it is the very mural that adorned the room two centuries ago.

People say that Betty Radcliffe remains in room 10 as well. Like the mural, she is faded, less vibrant, but she is still quite present in the love nest where she was murdered.

In the early 1990s, a couple who spent their wedding night in room 10 were kept awake by things other than the usual wedding night activities. At first, it was the continuous bother of footsteps that could be heard right outside their door. Then there were disembodied footsteps that could be heard inside the room. Finally at 3 AM, as the bride slept, the groom saw who it was who had been haunting them. As the room suddenly became ice cold, a dull orange light began to coalesce into a human figure in front of the mural. Slowly the glow materialized into the image of a woman in a white dress. The ghost paid no attention to her human company but turned with a blank expression and drifted silently toward the window. There, she vanished—leaving the room quiet for the remainder of the night. The next morning, there was a handprint marring the *inside* of the glass bolted over the mural.

Everyone agrees that the smudged handprint is Betty's calling card. Several people who have reported feeling ill at ease in the room have also reported mysterious prints on the inside of the glass. Guests always swear that the surface was clean when they checked into the room and agree that it would be impossible to create the illusion without removing the glass panes from the wall, which would be a daunting task.

Alan Simmonds, who works down the street at the Ancient House Museum, which was once Betty Radcliffe's home, recalled one couple who were particularly disturbed by the dirty fingerprints and all the activity that came with them.

In about 1992, Simmonds explained, "a couple came into the museum here, wanting to find out more about Betty Radcliffe. They were very frightened. They were on their honeymoon and they were staying in room 10.

"On their first night there, they had noticed that...old piece of decorated wall, which had been glazed over to stop people from touching it. Then, the following morning...they noticed that there were some handprints on the inside of the glass. They insisted that they had not been there the previous night.

"On their second night there, they said that the temperature had gone down very violently in the room, and that they had experienced strange happenings, such as the bedclothes being pulled off them during the night. They were very, very frightened and had decided to terminate their honeymoon at the Bell."

The newlyweds were not the only ones who found themselves unwilling to spend any more time than necessary with Betty. One manager of the hotel said that his dog, which roamed freely throughout the rest of the building, refused to cross the threshold of room 10. That same manager was once left speechless when a guest chose to go looking for other accommodations rather than take that room—the finest in the hotel—at a considerably discounted price. And there have been other guests in more recent years who have requested to be moved from Betty Radcliffe's room at the unlikely hour of 1 AM.

Not that Betty limits herself to frightening guests. Over the years, the staff have been targeted by her as well, particularly the chambermaids who tidy her room.

One maid claimed to have come out of the en suite to see a distinct impression in the shape of a body on the bed she had just freshly made up. Another spoke of the time she left her large bunch of keys in the lock—then saw them spin around twice of their own accord. A pair of women once addressed Betty jokingly when they had finished cleaning the room. They were answered with a sudden wave of bone-numbing cold. They ran from the room together, without bothering to say another word to Betty or each other. Also, according to Rachel Valentine, who works at the Bell's reception desk, "There is one housekeeping supervisor who has actually seen Betty!"

Valentine knows a number of the ghost stories about the hotel's former landlady and has even experienced a few odd occurrences herself.

"Our boss' office is beneath room 10," she said. "It's at the end of a long corridor. And when we have private meetings in there, we often can hear footsteps coming down the hallway. So we'll stop the meeting and wait, but no one ever actually appears at the door."

The window of room 10 looks across King Street to the 14th-century churchyard where Betty Radcliffe was supposedly laid to rest. However, Valentine, who is well-versed in both the legend and the ghost stories, couldn't confirm or deny that.

"We've been told that Betty is buried there," she said, "but nobody can actually find the gravestone."

Where Betty Radcliffe's earthly remains are may be a mystery—but there is little doubt where her spirit is. She haunts the scene of her life and death—the Bell Hotel in Thetford.

The End

Ghost House Books

Look for these volumes in our popular ghost story series:

Canadian Ghost Stories	1-55105-302-0
Even More Ghost Stories of Alberta	1-55105-323-3
Ghost Stories of California	1-55105-237-7
Ghost Stories of Hollywood	1-55105-241-5
Ghost Stories of Texas	1-55105-330-6
Ghost Stories of the Rocky Mountains	1-55105-165-6
Ghosts, Werewolves, Witches and Vampires	1-55105-333-0
More Ghost Stories of Saskatchewan	1-55105-276-8
Ontario Ghost Stories, Vol. I	1-55105-203-2

Coming soon...

Watch for these upcoming volumes from Ghost House Books:

Campfire Ghost Stories	1-894877-02-0
Ghost Stories of Indiana	1-894877-06-3
Ghost Stories of Michigan	1-894877-05-5
Ghost Stories of the Maritimes, Vol. II	1-894877-01-2
A Haunted Country Christmas	1-894877-15-2
Haunted Theaters	1-894877-04-7
Ontario Ghost Stories, Vol. II	1-894877-14-4

Available from your local bookseller.

For more information, contact our customer service department. In the United States, call 1-800-518-3541. In Canada, call 1-800-661-9017.